Anderson + Duchovny

An Extraordinary Story

DAVID BASSOM

HAMLYN

The author would like to thank the following extraordinary individuals for their encouragement, support and kindness: Julian Brown; Mike Evans, Tessa, Michael and Danny O'Brien; Mike Campbell-Montgomery; Terry and Doris McMahon; and Bridget Cunningham.

Photographic Acknowledgements

Front jacket: **Ronald Grant Archive**
Back jacket left to right: **Corbis-Bettmann/Everett Collection, Ronald Grant Archive, Alpha.**

Alpha 18, 19, 25, 47 bottom, 54 bottom, 56 bottom, 66 bottom, 76 top.
Aquarius Picture Library 42.
Brian Aris 2/3, 68/69, 78/79.
Courtesy of the **British Broadcasting Corporation** 71.
Corbis-Bettmann/Everett Collection 5, 5 bottom left, 8, 20/21, 23 bottom, 24, 29 top, 32 top, 50, 52, 53, 54 top, 55, 58/59, 60, 61, 62, 65, 72, 74, 77, 80.
Famous Scott Alonzo 12 top, Hubert Boesl 23 top, 67.
Courtesy of **FHM Magazine** 76 bottom.
Ronald Grant Archive 20 bottom, 20 top, 22 top, 22 bottom, 30/31.
Katz Compix 9 top, Outline/Karen Moskowitz 4 centre, 5 top left, Outline/Jim McHugh 13, Outline/Karen Moskowitz 16, 26, Norman NG 10 bottom, Outline/Jim McHugh 47 top, Alex Shaftel 70, Outline/Cesare Zucca 45.
Photofest 15, 29 bottom.
Pictorial Press Courtesy of Polygram 28, 32 bottom.
Retna Mark Anderson 11, Guy Aroch 37, 39 top, 39 bottom, 43, 44, Steve Granitz 64 top, Dan Howell 10 top, Patsy Lynch 64 bottom, Joe Marzullo 9 bottom, Bruce Malone 40/41, 46, 75, Gregory Pace 33, Richard Saputo 66 top.
Rex Features 4 bottom, 4 top, 5 top right, 6, 12 bottom, 14, 34, 36/37, 38 bottom, 38 top, 48, 51, 56/57, 56 top.

Publishing Director Laura Bamford
Executive Editor Julian Brown
Project Editor Mike Evans
Assistant Editor Karen O'Grady
Production Josephine Allum
Picture Research Wendy Gay
Design Steve Byrne

1/Generation X

2/Dreams, Drama and Day Jobs

5/X for Success

1/Generation X

The story behind Gillian Anderson and David Duchovny's rise to fame is almost worthy of an 'X-File' of its own

At the beginning of 1994, David Duchovny and Gillian Anderson were simply the leading actors of a little-known cult science fiction television series called *The X-Files.* By the end of 1995, they had been transformed into international superstars and were widely regarded as television's hottest double act.

Thanks to the phenomenal and wholly unexpected success of *The X-Files,* David Duchovny and Gillian Anderson have now become household names around the world and are currently more popular in their own right than most television shows. Although TV stars are generally considered to be the poor relations of film stars, this dynamic duo are the exception to the rule: both actors live in a constant media spotlight; they can command the covers of numerous magazines ranging from *Entertainment Weekly* and *The Radio Times* to *Rolling Stone* and *Details;* their faces adorn countless posters, books, T-Shirts, mugs, jigsaws and other such *X-Files* merchandising spin-offs; and production of *The X-Files* has been altered on several occasions to suit its leading actors' private lives and career goals.

Perhaps even more remarkably, both Duchovny and Anderson's characters in *The X-Files,* FBI Special Agents Fox Mulder and Dana Scully respectively, have slowly developed into unlikely icons of popular culture. More than any other film, TV show, play, book or real-life event, *The X-Files* have made it totally respectable to believe in extraterrestrial, supernatural and paranormal activity. Furthermore, the show has added considerable weight to global conspiracy theories. Consequently, wherever there is a mystery concerning unexplained phenomena or covert government activity, *X-File* fans (the

so-called X-philes) immediately envisage Mulder and Scully embarking on a quest for 'The Truth' behind the incident.

The X-Files is not only incredibly popular with TV audiences around the world but has also won widespread critical acclaim. One of the most atmospheric, intelligent and influential shows of the Nineties, *The X-Files* has received numerous accolades including a prestigious Golden Globe Award for Best Dramatic Series. David Duchovny and Gillian Anderson have themselves both been nominated for Emmy Awards, and Anderson collected the 1995 Screen Actors' Guild Award for Best Actress.

Yet ironically, neither Duchovny nor Anderson expected *The X-Files* to last more than a year and almost missed out on the opportunity to star in the show. When series creator/executive producer Chris Carter was casting the two lead roles, Duchovny was on the verge of movie stardom and was less than enthusiastic about the prospect of committing himself to a television series. Meanwhile, Anderson was primarily interested in stage or film roles, and had virtually no experience of working in the television industry.

The course of events surrounding the launch of *The X-Files* becomes even more extraordinary if you consider that neither of its stars showed any passion for acting during the early parts of their lives. Thus, it would

Neither Gillian Leigh Anderson nor David William Duchovny wanted to act when they were growing up

▶▶

A brilliant student, Duchovny won a scholarship to New York's Collegiate School before attending Princeton University

almost seem as if there were unexplained forces at work when David Duchovny and Gillian Anderson pursued the series of choices which ultimately led to their assignment to *The X-Files*.

As the senior member of *The X-Files* crew, David William Duchovny was born on August 7th, 1960 in New York City. The son of Scottish-American schoolteacher Margaret Ducovny and Jewish-American publicist Amram Ducovny, David was named after his father's favourite sculpture, Michelangelo's David. His mother provided David's middle name, William, as a tribute to her father.

Prior to David's birth, Amram decided to add the 'h' to his surname because he was tired of hearing his family name, 'Ducovny', mispronounced. Consequently, while his parents and older brother Danny all used 'Ducovny' as their surnames, both David and his younger sister Laurie were christened 'Duchovny'. Although David believes that Duchovny – and, for that matter, Ducovny – is a 'beautiful name', he has always been completely relaxed about the way it is pronounced (or mispronounced). Instead, he is more interested in the word's origin and meaning; whenever the topic is broached, he proudly points out that the name derived from a Russian word for 'spiritual'.

David Duchovny grew up in New York on 11th Street and 2nd Avenue. In true X-Files style, his family home was right across from a graveyard! Duchovny was a quiet and shy child at Elementary School; in fact, he was so quiet that his older brother Danny often told people that he was actually retarded! During his early school years, the timid student showed absolutely no interest in acting and was completely indifferent about his stage debut as one of the three magi in a school nativity play.

Duchovny once tried to evaluate the influence of his Scottish and Jewish heritage, and said that he inherited a 'Protestant work ethic combined with Jewish guilt and introspection' from his parents. He also quipped that no one should ever ask him for money!

He was probably also affected – on a subconscious level at least – by his father's experiences as a writer. Amram Ducovny had several books published, including *The Wisdom Of Spiro T. Agnew* and *David Ben-Gurion In His Own Words*, and also wrote an off-Broadway play, *The Trial Of Lee Harvey Oswald*. However, his youngest son wasn't particularly impressed by his fathers first (and last) effort as a playwright.

'It was really long,' Duchovny later told *Time Out*. 'Oswald just sat there and didn't say anything for the whole first act. I remember asking my father how it was possible that he didn't have to go to the bathroom!'

Sadly, watching *The Trial Of Lee Harvey Oswald* was not the worst experience of Duchovny's childhood. That came when he was eleven years old and forced to deal with the break-up of his parents' marriage. Many years later, Duchovny referred to their divorce as the 'most important emotional moment' of his childhood and revealed that he was forced into an 'adult world of emotions' that he was not prepared to deal with. He also felt that this painful event played a crucial role in defining the way he dealt with love throughout his life and might explain why he is perceived as a detached and morose individual by many of those around him.

Following the divorce, Margaret won custody of her family and started teaching at an elementary school to help financially support her children. David remained friends with his father and saw him on an occasional basis.

Margaret's biggest fear was that her children would end up penniless, so she encouraged them to work hard at school. Her efforts paid off in 1973, when David won a scholarship to New York's Collegiate School, an elite private boys' school whose students included the likes of John F. Kennedy Jr. and several actors-to-be, including Zach Gilligan (of *Gremlins* fame), Billy Wirth (*Body Snatchers*, and Duchovny's own series, *Red Shoe Diaries*) and Jason Beghe (*Thelma And Louise*, *Monkey Shines* and an early episode of *The X-Files*, 'Darkness Falls').

'I remember thinking I'll
never be this smart again'

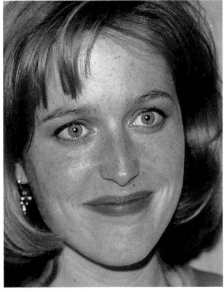

Top: Duchovny was working on his PhD at Yale when he was bitten by the acting bug

Above: Gillian Anderson was raised in Britain from the age of two, where she was teased and bullied because of her American accent

For David Duchovny, his scholarship to Collegiate School was nothing short of an introduction to a 'different world' – the world of high society. He would always remember visiting one of his privileged classmates at his apartment because it represented the first time he had ever used a private elevator! At school, he was known by the nicknames 'Duke' or 'Doggie' to his friends.

During the first year of his scholarship, Duchovny started seeing his first 'serious girl-friend'. The young couple dated for four years before they eventually decided to go their separate ways. Looking back at their relationship, Duchovny said that they might have stayed together and even got married if he had met her a little later in life.

Upon graduating from High School, Duchovny won a place at Princeton University to study English. While many of his class-mates seized the opportunity to go wild and 'party down' in classic University tradition, Duchovny devoted most of his time to study and was, by his own admission, one of the institution's most 'tight-assed' students. Duchovny worked particularly hard on his senior thesis, which was entitled, 'The Schizophrenic Critique of Pure Reason in Beckett's Early Novels', while his few plea-sures in life included baseball, basketball, swimming and yoga.

Duchovny discovered the delights of vegetarianism and *Star Trek* at Princeton. However, as much as he enjoyed the adven-tures of William Shatner, Leonard Nimoy et al, he never really considered pursuing a career as an actor. In fact, when he discovered that one of his roommates intended to act profes-sionally once he had completed his education, Duchovny told him: 'You came to Princeton. Why are you acting?'

After successfully completing his degree, Duchovny decided to stay at Yale to study for a Master of Arts in English Literature. His strongest memory of this period of his life was of the immense amount of time he spent preparing for his oral examination. 'In the four months before my opals, I read maybe eight, nine hours a day – maybe more,' Duchovny told *The Boston Globe*. 'The day before, my head felt heavy, like it would roll off my shoul-ders. . . I remember thinking, "I'll never be this smart again."'

Margaret Ducovny was delighted when her son won his MA and convinced him to study for his PhD, after which he could work as a university lecturer. Duchovny soon started researching his dissertation, 'Magic and Technology in Contemporary Poetry and Prose', which was inspired by Richard Rorty's review of Christopher Lasch in *The New Yorker* entitled 'The Culture of Narcissism'. While writing his PhD, Duchovny supported himself by working as a teaching assistant. Norman Mailer, Elmore Leonard and Thomas Pynchon were just some of his favourite authors at the time, and his classmates included such up-and-coming American writ-ers as Harold Bloom, John Hollander, Jay Hillis Miller and Geoffrey Hartman.

Although he enjoyed reading and writing, Duchovny never really felt like an academic and increasingly resented the prospect of spending the rest of his life as a teacher 'cod-dled in an unreal word.' He slowly came to the conclusion that he would like to write profes-sionally, and felt that the best way to learn about the art of writing was to study the clas-sics as part of his PhD.

In 1985, one of Duchovny's friends told him that he should take up acting as a hobby. Having grown bored with academic life, Duchovny thought that it might be a good way to learn more about writing and decided to give it a try. After spending a few hours with the Yale Drama School, the PhD student's atti-tude and outlook suddenly changed. Much to his surprise, Duchovny found that acting pro-vided him with 'an emotional life' for the first time in his existence. He could also detect a sense of teamwork between the actors and the production crew which reminded him of team sport, and thus was something he really liked. This simply discovery would alter the course of Duchovny's life forever, and spell the end of his promising academic career.

David Duchovny's upbringing and road to the stage seems straightforward when com-pared to that of his *X-Files* co-star, Gillian Leigh Anderson. Born on August 9th, 1968 at St. Mary's Hospital, Cook County, Chicago, Gillian was the first-born child of Edward and Rosemary Anderson. Shortly after her birth, the Andersons spent some time in Puerto Rico before they moved to Britain in 1970, where Edward studied at the London Film

School. Edward once said of this period, 'We had hardly any money and they were quite tough times for the family'.

At the age of five, Gillian Anderson started to attend the Coleridge Junior School in Crouch End, north London. Unfortunately for her, she had picked up an American accent from her parents. As soon as her young classmates heard her speak, they started to abuse and taunt her. Gillian was also bullied, until she learned to fight back.

In 1979, the Anderson family decided to leave Britain and moved to Grand Rapids, Michigan, where Gillian completed her primary school education at the Fountain Elementary before enrolling at Michigan's City High School. Sadly, Gillian's fortunes did not change for the better. After six difficult years of study in London, she considered herself to be effectively British and had difficulty adjusting to being back in America. Once again, she was teased for her trans-Atlantic accent which nobody in her class could understand. As a result, she felt 'unpopular' and became 'withdrawn' at school.

Things went from bad to worse as far as Gillian was concerned when her parents revealed that new members of the family were

Anderson considered herself to be British when she returned to America, and was once again teased and bullied by her classmates

▶ ▶

During her time at Michigan, Anderson was voted 'most bizarre girl', 'class clown', 'most likely to go bald' and 'most likely to be arrested' by her classmates.

on the way. 1981 marked the birth of her sister, Zoe, while her brother Aaron joined the family in 1984. Anderson quickly became jealous of her younger siblings and yearned to be the centre of her parents' attention again.

Anderson's pain led her to rebel against the system in the archetypal James Dean mode. She swiftly shed her image as 'a good little girl in corduroys and plaid' and brought punk to Michigan. Inspired by her time in London, Anderson dyed her hair, put a stud in her left nostril, had a three-foot purple mohican and wore $2 dresses. Consequently, she emerged as a cross between Madonna and Johnny Rotten, and she even developed a requisite taste in punk music; her favourite pop groups at the time were The Circle Jerks, The Dead Kennedys and Elvis Costello.

'I did it to express my anger,' she later explained, 'because I had a lot of it and I was never very good at dealing with my emotions.'

At school, Anderson's grades plummeted as she focused her energies on swearing, daydreaming, pulling pranks, talking and throwing paper aeroplanes. She was frequently sent to see the school's headmaster, who would reprimand her for her rowdy and disobedient behaviour.

Anderson embarked on her first serious relationship with a punk who apparently went on to became a Neo-Nazi. The following year, she became involved with a penniless punk musician ten years older than her, and of no fixed abode. Whenever they chose to stay together, the less-than-happy couple would sleep rough in warehouses and on friends' apartment floors.

Many years later, Anderson described this part of her life as being 'excruciatingly painful'. She was promiscuous and apparently enjoyed drinking and taking drugs because at that time, 'Anything and every-

thing was fair game.' Although her parents were troubled by their elder daughter's behaviour, they decided not take a confrontational stance against her, but instead gave Gillian the freedom to sort out her own problems and pursue her independence.

As a child, Anderson had always wanted to be a marine biologist, a geologist or an archaeologist when she grew up. However, all her ambitions faded away during her rebellious adolescence. During her time at Michigan, the teenage tearaway was voted 'most bizarre girl', 'class clown', 'most likely to go bald' and 'most likely to be arrested' by her classmates.

Ironically, she fulfilled one of their expectations on graduation night, when she was caught trying to break into high school with a group of friends. Anderson had hoped to glue all the locks inside the building as a practical joke, so that no-one could enter the school's classrooms the following day. However, she was somewhat intoxicated at the time, and just could not crack the locks on the school's front door. After a while, her boyfriend and most of her friends decided to give up, but Anderson was determined to complete her mission. She struggled alone with the locks until a passing group of police saw what was going on and wasted no time in arresting her. Gillian was finger-printed and photographed for police records before her boyfriend arrived and provided bail.

Luckily for her, Gillian's rebellious phase came to an abrupt end shortly after, when she attended a couple of auditions at the Grand Rapids Community Theatre. Although she had little interest in acting and agreed to audition 'just for the hell of it', she immediately 'felt at home' on stage. As a result, her outlook changed and she found a calling in life. Gillian Anderson wanted to be an actress.

A troubled teenager, Anderson became a one of Michigan's first punks and ultimately found herself on the wrong side of the law. What would Dana Scully say?

▶▶

2/Dreams, Drama and Day Jobs

2/Dreams, Drama and Day Jobs

Both Duchovny and Anderson made slow starts to their careers and had to rely on part-time jobs to keep their dreams alive

After studying at the Actors' Studio David Duchovny made his inauspicious screen debut in a Lowenbrau beer commercial

D avid Duchovny was still studying for his PhD at Yale when he was bitten by the acting bug. Not long after his first few sessions with the University Drama Class, he started commuting to New York to perform in coffee-house theatres on the Lower East Side. Duchovny subsequently won a part-time place at the acclaimed Actors' Studio in New York City, where he studied under Marsha Haufrecht.

Whilst attending the Actors' Studio, Duchovny developed the basis of his distinctive style of performing, which has tended to divide critical opinion: some reviewers perceive his work as being intuitive and charismatic; others find him incredibly stiff and somewhat wooden.

Essentially, Haufrecht taught her young student that the key to being a good actor is honesty. Consequently, if an actor feels that an action does not suit the character, the performer should just improvise the correct response because, as far as Duchovny is concerned, improvisation is a vital tool of staying true to the character. Thus, for example, if a performer is participating in a funeral scene and feels likes giggling, then the actor should giggle because that is the best way to stay true to the character! Duchovny also learned that carefully-planned, intellectual performances are generally extremely boring for an audience to watch, and chose to place his trust in instinctive acting.

Duchovny appeared in numerous plays during his time in New York, and adapted Charles Bukowski's play, *The Copulating Mermaid of Venice Beach* for a 'Way-Off

Broadway' stage production. The PhD student-turned-actor/writer quickly developed a love for stage work, which he described as 'pure bliss'.

In 1987, Duchovny's old school friend Jason Beghe contacted him with a idea that would change his career – and, indeed, his entire life. Beghe had recently made his screen debut in the Susan Sarandon film *Compromising Positions* and suggested that he should audition for a beer commercial, which would provide him with extra income. Despite his love for the theatre, Duchovny had never ruled out the possibility of television and film roles, and discussed the idea with his then-girlfriend, aspiring actress Maggie Wheeler (who later played a recurring role in the smash-hit sitcom *Friends*). Wheeler assured him that appearing in a commercial wouldn't damage his career and would be an easy money-spinner.

After several auditions, Duchovny landed the starring role in a Lowenbrau beer commercial. When the day of the filming arrived, he was extremely nervous and even fluffed his lines during the first two takes! After that, however, there was no stopping him and the

Dreams, Drama And Day Jobs

Top: **Duchovny with cult filmmaker Henry Jaglom who re-wrote the role of Billy in** *New Year's Day* **to suit Duchovny**

Above: **Upon landing the role in the arthouse flick** *New Year's Day***, Duchovny quit his PhD and turned his back on his academic career**

commercial was completed without incident. Duchovny earned $9,000 for his work in the advert, which was more than what he earned as a teaching assistant in a whole year!

Following his screen debut, Duchovny was invited to audition for no less than three pilots for potential television series. The auditions were scheduled to take place during holiday time at Yale, so he agreed to attend. As soon as he confirmed his availability, Duchovny was promptly flown to Los Angeles, where he stayed at the upmarket Sunset Marquis Hotel and was driven everywhere by limo. The PhD student was amazed by just how lucrative and comfortable the acting profession could be! When his auditions were delayed and continued into term time, Duchovny phoned in sick – from the poolside of his luxury hotel!

Although Duchovny ultimately didn't win any of the roles he auditioned for, his experience in Los Angeles taught him that he would have to quit Yale if he wanted to pursue an acting career properly. Consequently, as soon as he won a lead role in a low-budget film, *New Year's Day*, Duchovny decided to drop out. His family were surprised by his decision, particularly his mother Margaret, who had always hoped that David would become a University lecturer and felt particularly disappointed that he brought his excellent academic career to a premature end.

New Year's Day was written and directed by cult filmmaker Henry Jaglom, whose credits included *Someone to Love*, *Can She Bake a Cherry Pie?* and *Sitting Ducks*, as well as two movies in the *National Lampoon* series. An angst-ridden domestic drama firmly in the Woody Allen mould, the film focuses on a group of New Yorkers who pour out their heart's desire to one another on (no prizes for guessing!) New Year's Day. Duchovny plays the movie's leading man, Billy, a sleazy smooth-talking romeo who tries to seduce Annie (Gwen Welles) and Winona (Melanie Winter), before being caught by his girlfriend Lucy (Maggie Jackobson).

Jaglom re-wrote Duchovny's role to suit him, and the actor improvised a great deal of his dialogue because he felt that he wasn't experienced enough to bring Jaglom's script to life. The film also required Duchovny to appear naked in the scene in which Billy is

thrown out of his apartment. Fortunately, David didn't have any qualms about being on screen nude and has always been willing to bare all for his art, provided that it was an essential element of the script and wasn't in any way gratuitous.

Once *New Year's Day* was completed, Duchovny took the advice of his agent and moved to Los Angeles to pursue his career and see if *New Year's Day* created 'any heat'. Unfortunately, Jaglom ran into financial problems shortly before the movie's release, which meant that *New Year's Day* didn't see the light of day until 1989.

With only a beer commercial and a film that nobody had seen to his credit, Duchovny was hardly considered a 'hot property' by Hollywood casting agents. Apart from a few more commercials, Duchovny couldn't win any more acting roles and soon turned to other professions to make a living. Whilst waiting for the role that would put his career back on track, he wrote magazine articles and worked as a caterer and a barman.

Duchovny would later refer to this lull in his career as the 'hardest time' of his life. He was wracked with self-doubt and questioned whether or not he should have left Yale. He was also annoyed that all his hard work at Princeton and Yale seemed to count for nothing: casting agents weren't interested in his academic achievements and always seemed to focus on his lack of acting experience.

In 1988, Duchovny won a small role in the film *Working Girl*, Mike Nichols' big-budget reworking of *Cinderella* starring Melanie Griffith as aspiring businesswoman Tess McGill, Sigourney Weaver as her scheming boss Katherine Parker and Harrison Ford as the *Prince Charming* of the piece, Jack Trainer. David Duchovny appears briefly in the film during Tess' Birthday Party, and is imagi-

▶▶

Dreams, Drama
And Day Jobs

Above: Duchovny turns on the charm with co-star Daphna Kastner as telephone hustler Daniel in *Julia Has Two Lovers*

natively listed in the credits as 'Tess' Birthday Party Friend'! Nevertheless, *Working Girl* featured an all-star cast, won mild critical acclaim and was a smash hit at the box office, so the film went nicely on his resume.

Unfortunately, his presence in the film wasn't enough to revitalise his career and he didn't act professionally until the following year, when he landed an equally small role in the film *Bad Influence*. David Duchovny can be seen drinking in the background while Rob Lowe and James Spader begin their battle of wills, and is described simply as 'club goer' in the credits.

Duchovny's big break finally came in 1990, when he won a recurring role in the second (and last) season of *Twin Peaks*. David Lynch's cult TV series gave Duchovny his first taste of *X-Files*-style story-telling and also provided him with the experience of playing his first FBI agent. Unlike Fox Mulder, however, Duchovny's character in *Twin Peaks* had little time for unexplained phenomena and government conspiracies. Instead, he was much more interested in which dress and high heels suited him.

The colourful character of DEA Agent Dennis/Denise Bryson was loosely inspired by former FBI chief J. Edgar Hoover and required Duchovny to make his debut as a transvestite. Although such a role might be considered too risky by most aspiring leading men, Duchovny never once thought that his work in *Twin Peaks* might hamper his career in any way. He was simply overjoyed that he had won a 'cool part' in a 'cool show'. And besides, he still needed the money.

Ever since he played Dennis/Denise Bryson, Duchovny has repeatedly been asked what he thought of cross-dressing. The actor invariably replies that he liked it more than he can say! On a more serious note, he also normally says that he can't believe how hard it is to wear womens' clothing and really appreciates not having to wear a bra all of the time. Duchovny believes that he makes an unattractive woman, but had been told on many occasions that he had nice legs; in fact, his

sister told him she was jealous of his pins after seeing an episode of *Twin Peaks*!

Dennis/Denise Bryson featured in just three episodes of *Twin Peaks*, but almost certainly would have returned had the show not been cancelled at the end of its second year. In any case, the role was enough to generate a lot of interest in David Duchovny and his agent was inundated with film and TV roles.

Consequently, 1991 represented an extremely busy twelve months for the promising actor. He started the year with a substantial role in *The Rapture*, an unrelenting and disturbing pseudo-religious drama. The film marked the directorial debut of Michael Tolkin, and follows a young woman's tragic journey from aethism to religious fanaticism.

By day, Sharon (Mimi Rogers of *Someone To Watch Over Me* fame) spends her time wasting away in her dead-end job. At night, she and her debauched boyfriend Vic (Patrick Bauchau) cruise the local clubs looking for new lovers. Gradually, however, Sharon grows tired of her unfocused and meaningless existence and she turns to organised religion to find the answer to her problems.

The story picks up six years later. Sharon is happily married to one of her old lovers, Randy (Duchovny), and together they are raising their daughter. However, Sharon's domestic bliss is shattered when Randy is killed by one of his colleagues at work, and she perceives her husband's death as a sign that the Day Of Judgement is nigh.

As Sharon, Mimi Rogers gives the finest performance in her career, while Duchovny manages to capture Randy's transformation from sleaze ball to respectable family man with ease. Ultimately, the film's uncompromising subject matter prevented it from reaching a mass audience, but it still enjoyed a successful run on the art house circuit and earned Duchovny some good reviews.

The actor was next seen in *Julia Has Two Lovers*, another art house movie directed by Bashar Shbib. An offbeat romantic comedy, the film stars Duchovny as Daniel, a telephone hustler who calls women at random and seduces them. One morning, he calls a single young woman named Julia (Daphna Kastner) and they swiftly embark on a passionate affair – despite the fact that she is already dating Jack (David Charles).

Julia Has Two Lovers was widely described as an amateurish and instantly forgettable affair by most critics, and barely managed to recoup its meagre cost at the box office. Despite a strong central performance from Kastner and the film's vaguely promising premise, the screenplay (written, incidentally, by Shbib and Kastner) neglects to develop the idea and fails to keep the audience's attention throughout the course of proceedings.

David Duchovny won mixed reviews for his role in the film; *The New York Times* summed up most critics' reactions by concluding that the actor projected 'an agreeable, low-keyed self-assurance'. Duchovny himself felt that the film was below par, but said that he enjoyed making it immensely because it was mostly improvised, and thus suited his acting style. The actor was particularly pleased with the scene in which his character makes his initial call to Julia, as the (largely improvised) dialogue flows very naturally and seems very believable.

Sadly, most of his co-stars and the film's production crew didn't share his enthusiasm for the project. In fact, Duchovny admitted that he could often hear people snoring as several of the film's key sequences were shot!

It was around this time that Duchovny met his long-time girlfriend, actress Perrey Reeves. He was trying to decide between a blue and a grey suit in a clothing boutique when he caught sight of Perrey and immediately wanted to get to know her. In a blatant attempt to strike up a conversation, he asked her which suit he should buy. She told him to buy both and the rest, as they say, is history.

Following the completion of *Julia Has Two Lovers*, Duchovny started work on the his most commercial film to date, the teen-orientated black comedy *Don't Tell Mom The Babysitter's Dead*. Essentially a vehicle for up-and-coming starlet Christina Applegate (best

known for her role in Fox's immensely popular US sitcom *Married... With Children*), the film follows the adventures of a group of teenagers who have to fend for themselves during a summer holiday when their babysitter dies of a sudden coronary.

Don't Tell Mom The Babysitter's Dead, was a resounding flop at the box office and spelt the end of Applegate's film career. Luckily, David Duchovny's role as Bruce was so brief that he emerged unscathed from the celluloid catastrophe.

Duchovny returned to the world of modest film-making for his next effort, *Denial: The Dark Side of Passion*. Written and directed by Eric Dignam, the movie follows a battle for supremacy between two lovers (played by Robin Wright and Jason Patrick) and features Duchovny in another supporting role as John.

However, 1991 proved to be David Duchovny's busiest year as an actor. After a troubled start to his career, he had demonstrated an ability to alternate between leading and supporting roles in a diverse range of projects and was clearly not afraid of taking risks. In short, his star was in ascent. And it didn't look like he would have to work as a journalist, caterer or barman for some time to come!

Ironically, while Duchovny found that he had to 'quit thinking' to be a successful actor, Gillian Anderson worked harder than she ever had at school to become an actress. Upon graduating from Michigan City High School, she moved to Chicago where she attended Goodman Theater School at DePaul University and gained a Bachelor of Fine Arts (BFA) degree. As a keen drama student, Anderson felt inspired and wanted to do as well as she possibly could.

In 1988, she attended the Summer programme at the National Theatre of Great Britain at Cornell University, New York, to gain further experience of her craft. The following year, she decided to quit drinking, because she enjoyed alcohol 'a bit too much' and did not want anything to hamper her work. Anderson took her last tipple before her 21st birthday, and never broke her pledge.

Top: **Duchovny started dating actress Perrey Reeves after a chance meeting in a clothing boutique**

Above: **Don't Tell Mom The Babysitter's Dead' featured Duchovny as the slimy businessman Bruce**

Dreams, Drama And Day Jobs

Upon moving to New York, Gillian Anderson vowed never to work in the television industry or move to Los Angeles

Anderson performed in numerous stage productions at the Goodman Theater School, and her very favourite was a farce called *A Flea In Her Ear*. Although she only had a very small role, she enjoyed the play because it represented her first attempt at comedy.

During her time in Chicago, Anderson was noticed by a talent scout from the all-powerful William Morris Agency. The organisation promptly offered to represent her if she moved to New York. Naturally, if was an offer the aspiring actress couldn't refuse.

Thus, at eleven o'clock one night, she loaded her Volkswagen with all her worldly goods and headed straight for the 'Big Apple'. 'The car was packed so high that I couldn't see out the rear-view mirror,' she recalled. 'And when I stopped to sleep, I had to crouch up in a foetal position.'

Once in New York, Anderson swore that she would never move to Los Angeles or pursue television roles. She simply wanted to perform on the stage and, if necessary, on film. Despite the support of the William Morris Agency, however, roles were initially few and far between and Anderson had to work as a waitress to support herself.

Gillian Anderson's career as a waitress came to an extremely sudden (but temporary) end in 1991, when Mary-Louise Parker suddenly dropped out of the leading female role in an off-Broadway production of Alan Ayckbourne's *Absent Friends*, two weeks into rehearsals. Parker had been offered a part in the Lawrence Kasdan movie *Grand Canyon* and left the producers frantically searching for a replacement. After several auditions, Anderson was eventually chosen to replace Parker and went on to collect rave reviews as well as a prestigious Theater World Award for her performance.

Unfortunately, acclaim and accolades do not pay the bills and as soon as *Absent Friends* came to a close, Anderson found herself out of work again. After a couple of weeks of unemployment, she was forced to work as a waitress in two different places to make ends meet. A few months later, in keeping with the old adage that it never rains but it pours, she was offered roles in no less than three

projects all on the same day: the first part was in another off-Broadway play in New York; the second was in a production of Christopher Hampton's *The Philanthropist* at the Long Wharf Theatre in New Haven, Connecticut; and the third was in a low-budget feature film, *Home Fires Burning*.

After a lot of thought, Anderson realised that if she declined the opportunity to star in the New York play, she could film her role in *Home Fires Burning* before starting work on *The Philanthropist*.

An adaptation of Chris Ceraso's play, *Home Fires Burning* explores the resurgence of fascism and its affect on everyday life. The film begins with troubled 22-year-old Clifford Harnish (Michael Dolan) returning home after several years of travelling, only to discover that his father, Mark Harnish (Raymond J. Barry) is having an affair with another woman, Glory (Karen Allen of *Raiders Of The Lost Ark*, fame) while his mother Martha (Tess Harper) has become an alcoholic. After trying to talk his father into dumping Glory, the deeply right-wing Clifford confronts her and threatens her with violence unless she agrees to leave.

Directed by L. A. Puopolo, *Home Fires Burning* fails to transcend its theatrical roots and lacks any visceral or emotional impact. Nevertheless, the film's cast won some respectable notices, including Gillian Anderson in her movie debut as Clifford's girlfriend, April Cavanaugh.

Home Fires Burning was given a brief theatrical release, but unfortunately failed to recoup it losses. Eventually, it was retitled *The Turning* and broadcast on the US cable TV network HBO. Anderson herself later dismissed the film and told X-philes not to waste their time trying to find it!

Straight after she had finished working on *Home Fires Burning*, Anderson returned to the stage to start work on *The Philanthropist* in New Haven. The production was a modest success and won the actress further praise, but once again did little for her career. Indirectly, however, *The Philanthropist* was destined to play a crucial role in sending Gillian Anderson to Los Angeles – and towards the television industry.

▶▶

3/Worlds Apart

As Duchovny drew closer to movie stardom, Anderson's career suffered a minor setback

Twin Peaks **prevented David Duchovny's acting career from coming to a premature end and helped him land no less than four film roles in 1991. The following twelve months proved equally productive for the up-and-coming movie star.**

Duchovny started 1992 by returning to the art house circuit for director Henry Jaglom's *Venice/Venice*. A ridiculously egotistical affair, the film stars Jaglom as a maverick American director, Dean, and Nelly Alard as a French journalist who becomes completely obsessed

with his work. Duchovny played a brief supporting role as Dylan and enjoyed being reunited with Jaglom (with whom he had worked on *New Year's Day*) and Daphna Kastner (the female lead in *Julia Has Two Lovers*).

few days a month, or could even be shot in one block over the course of a few weeks), he realised that the series would provide him with an element of security without restricting him from working in other projects.

In the opening instalment of *The Red Shoe Diaries*, Jake (Duchovny) is shocked by the sudden and unexpected suicide of his fiancee. Distraught and confused by her death, the wimpy architect starts to read her diary and is stunned to learn that his girlfriend was having an affair. Jake vows that he will not allow a similar tragedy to befall anyone else and places an advert in a newspaper in which he asks people to share their innermost secrets with him.

Thus, Duchovny serves as the narrator of the romantic anthology series, and plays the show's only recurring character. Like in *The X-Files*, Duchovny seldom has any opportunity for romance in the series. As the actor himself often admitted, 'Everybody else gets the girl on that show.'

Once Duchovny had finished shooting the first segments of *The Red Shoe Diaries*, he was free to pursue other roles and was cast in Richard Attenborough's lavish biopic, *Chaplin*. Whilst the epic film was a powerful showcase for Robert Downey Jr. as the legendary comedian and featured a truly enormous cast, Duchovny had a few nice moments as camera man Rollie Totheroh and felt honoured to be associated with such a prestigious project.

Duchovny's next movie, *Beethoven*, proved to be the biggest money-spinner of his career. The light-hearted comedy follows the Newton family's attempts to come to terms with an unwanted guest – the eponymous Beethoven, a 185-pound St. Bernard. Despite the presence of screen veteran Charles Grodin and Helen Hunt, the St. Bernard was the star of the show and made the movie into a box-office blockbuster. As the evil yuppie Brad, Duchovny was required to break his profession's golden rule and work with children and animals. He later told *Entertainment Weekly* that his most vivid memory of the film was that Beethoven 'had a lot of saliva.'

The actor returned to the world of television for his next project, the gripping telemovie *Baby Snatcher*. Based on a true story, Joyce Chopra's domestic drama

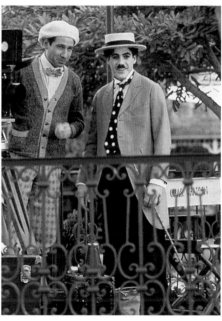

Opposite: **On the trail of a serial killer with Michelle Forbes in *Kalifornia***

*Top: **The Red Shoe Diaries** provided Duchovny with his first starring role in a television series*

Above: **Duchovny as cameraman Rollie Totheroh and Robert Downey Jr as Chaplin in Richard Attenborough's epic biopic**

The actor then accepted a minor part in John Mackenzie's controversial biopic *Ruby*. A semi-fictionalised account of the John F. Kennedy assassination from the perspective of Jack Ruby (Danny Aiello), the film featured Duchovny as police officer J. D. Tippit, whose main tasks were to lust after stripper Candy Cane (Sherilyn Fenn) and look uncomfortable in his police outfit!

After he had completed work on *Ruby*, Duchovny was then offered a regular role in a television series, *The Red Shoe Diaries*. Unfortunately, the actor had come to love moving between different roles in diverse projects, so he explained to the show's producers he that had little desire to be bound to a long-running TV series. However, when they told him that his part as the show's narrator would not be very demanding (it would take only a

Previous page: Duchovny falls under Sherilyn Fenn's spell in *Ruby*

Top: The smash-hit family comedy *Beethoven* featured Duchovny as the evil yuppie, Brad

Above: Brian Kessler (Duchovny) learns that his passenger Early Grayce (Brad Pitt) has something of an offbeat sense of humour in *Kalifornia*

Opposite: Following her Award-winning performance in the play *Absent Friends* and promising film debut, in *Home Fires Burning*, Gillian Anderson was forced to resume her career as a waitress whilst waiting for new projects to come her way!

Duchovny knew he would get another chance at the 'big time' and was willing to wait for it

toplines Veronica Hamel (of *Hill Street Blues* fame) as Bianca Hudson, a middle-aged woman who secretly kidnaps an unwed mother's child and attempts to raise it as her own. While Karen Williams (Nancy McKeon) searches for her baby, she realises that the FBI suspect her of killing the infant. Duchovny gives a strong performance as the child's father David Anderson, an affluent businessman torn between his wife and his secret family.

With a string of movie roles and a television series to his credit, David Duchovny's career was really beginning to take off. When the actor was cast opposite Hollywood superstar Brad Pitt (fresh from his success in *A River Run Through It*) and rising starlet Juliette Lewis (*Cape Fear*) in *Kalifornia*, it looked as if David Duchovny was about to break into Hollywood's 'A-List'.

The directorial debut of the pop video maestro Dominic Sena, *Kalifornia* opens with ambitious journalist Brian Kessler (Duchovny) and his photographer girlfriend Carrie (Michelle Forbes) embarking on a cross-country tour of historic murder sites to research their book on serial killers. Shortly into their drive, the couple decide that they should find some passengers to share their travel expenses with and subsequently pick up a charismatic stranger Early Grayce (Pitt) and his girlfriend Adele (Lewis).

As their journey continues, however, Brian and Carrie realise that they might have a real-life serial killer in the back seat of their car! Hopes were high for *Kalifornia*. On paper, the film just couldn't fail: the public's fascination with serial killers have been proven by the huge success of *Silence of the lambs*; road movies were always a popular staple of American film-making; and Brad Pitt was a hot property. Most Hollywood insiders expected it to be a solid box office hit.

They were wrong. Most critics condemned the film as a waste of time, and it proved to be a resounding flop at the box office. Even Brad Pitt's loyal fans chose to give it a miss, because they were unprepared to see their idol in the darkest (and least photogenic) role of his career.

Despite its harsh reception, however, *Kalifornia* isn't a total disaster. The four lead performances are uniformly excellent; Pitt is a revelation as the villain of the peace and David Duchovny acquits himself well as the film's 'everyman' character. Unfortunately, *Kalifornia* is let down by Dominic Sena's pretentious and superficial direction, which fails to grab viewers' attention and allows the purported 'ride into terror' to become a ride into tedium.

Kalifornia might not have transformed David Duchovny into a movie star, but it did illustrate that he was actually capable of playing leading roles in mainstream movies. Disappointed but not deterred, Duchovny knew that he would get another chance at the 'big time' and was willing to wait for it.

As David Duchovny's career soared to new heights, Gillian Anderson wasn't so lucky and found that roles were increasingly few and far between. Following the completion of *The Philanthropist* in New Haven, the acclaimed actress faced another prolonged period of unemployment. After a while, she decided to travel to Los Angeles to visit an actor she'd become romantically-involved with during her work in New Haven.

During her stay, Anderson's boyfriend convinced Anderson to stay in Los Angeles on the grounds that there were more acting opportunities in and around Hollywood than there were in New York. Despite her vow never to move to L.A., Anderson decided to stay there for a while and her host agreed to financially support her until she found work.

On the first day of her job hunt in Los Angeles, Anderson swore to herself that she would never work on television. She had never really watched or cared for TV and was only interested in theatre and film roles. However, the actress soon changed her tune when she just couldn't land any stage and movie projects and was forced to resume her career as a waitress to fund herself.

Between 1991 and 1992, Gillian attended between an average of two or three auditions a day, to no avail. Eventually, she won a guest slot in the eighth episode of Fox TV's short-lived sitcom *Class of '96* entitled 'The Accused'. The show marked her television debut and was, incredibly, her only small screen credit prior to landing a starring role in *The X-Files*.

Anderson subsequently recorded an audiocassette adaptation of Anne Rice's novel *Exit to Eden*. She had just two days to read the book with another actor and hadn't realised that she was required to perform various accents, including South American and French! 'There wasn't any time to work on it,' she told Vancouver's CBC station many years later. 'It was mostly just diving in head-first and hoping that I didn't completely embarrass myself.' Following her rise to fame with *The X-Files*, Anderson was shocked to learn that the tape was still available and was actually selling fast to hungry X-philes around the world!

By the end of 1992, Gillian Anderson and David Duchovny were worlds apart. While for Duchovny, the future had never looked brighter, Anderson's career had reached a dead end. Both personally and professionally, their backgrounds and situations just could not have been any more diverse. However, their lives and careers were about to converge with the launch of a television series entitled *The X-Files*.

4/Opening the Files

When *The X-Files* entered production, few people expected it to last for more than a year

In the summer of 1992, 20th Century Fox executives started to consider potential ideas for the television shows which would form their Autumn 1993 schedule. One of the 37 premises vying for attention was an offbeat science fiction/ horror thriller series entitled *The X-Files*.

The X-Files was the brainchild of Chris Carter, a former journalist and one-time editor of *Surfing Magazine*, whose television credits included two highly successful comedy series, *Rags to Riches* and *Brand New Life*, as well as a failed pilot, *Cameo By Night*. Carter loosely based the show on the short-lived Seventies horror series *Kolchak: The Night Stalker*, and promised Fox that *The X-Files* would be stylish, sophisticated and extremely scary. The proposed series would follow the adventures of FBI Special Agents Fox Mulder and Dana Scully, who were assigned to shed light on various unsolved FBI cases involving unexplained phenomena – the so-called *X-Files* of the title.

To ensure that Mulder and Scully's battles against the likes of aliens, liver-eating monsters and shapeshifters never became laughable or too ridiculous, Carter stressed that the series would be shot in a very serious, almost documentary-style, and that everything that took place would fall into the realm of 'extreme possibility'; in other words, the

Opposite: Gillian Anderson and David Duchovny joined forces for the first time to work on the pilot of *The X-Files* in March 1993

Above: Like most of 20th Century Fox's television shows, *The X-Files* is filmed in Vancouver, Canada to keep production costs to a minimum

show's storylines might always seem improbable, but they would never be impossible.

Whilst developing the show, Carter realised that its audience would be divided into two groups: those who were willing to accept the existence of extraterrestrial, paranormal and supernatural phenomena; and those who were unconvinced. Consequently, he decided to make Fox Mulder a true believer and Dana Scully a sceptic who feels that everything ultimately has a scientific answer. As Carter pointed out, this would not only allow the show to accurately present two perspectives of each story, but also provide the basis of some strong conflict between the leading characters.

During an early discussion with Fox, it became clear that the studio felt that *The X-Files* premise was too restrictive. One executive pointed out that the similarly-themed *Kolchak: The Night Stalker* ran out of steam after half a season and swiftly became repetitive and boring. In a bid to assuage their doubts, Carter had the brilliant idea of adding a recurring subplot to *The X-Files*, concerning an international governmental conspiracy. This, of course, gave birth to the show's catchy taglines 'the truth is out there', 'trust no one' and 'I want to believe', which swiftly earned their places in popular culture.

Despite Carter's ambitious plans and breathless enthusiasm for *The X-Files* Fox executives were unconvinced that an audience existed for such an unusual project. Most of them felt that the show would at best emulate the success of *Twin Peaks*, which gained an extremely loyal audience but failed to break into the mainstream and was cancelled after just two years. At the same time, however, they were also aware of the remarkable critical and commercial success of the FBI/horror movie *The Silence of the Lambs* and wondered if *The X-Files* would have as wide an appeal. Eventually, they decided to commission a pilot episode of *The X-Files* to test the murky waters surrounding the genre.

Upon reading the description of FBI Special Agent Mulder, casting chief Randy Stone was quick to recommended David Duchovny to Chris Carter. Stone was aware of Duchovny's prospering movie career and also remembered his performance as the cross-dressing FBI agent Dennis/Denise Bryson in *Twin Peaks*.

Although *Kalifornia* hadn't been the box office smash everyone expected, Duchovny was still on the brink of movie stardom. All he needed was a substantial hit. Consequently, the actor had little interest in television projects, which would represent a step backwards in his career. Duchovny's manager would read every single script that was sent for his consideration and would then almost always decline the offer on behalf of her client.

However, *The X-Files* was the exception to the rule. As soon as she finished reading the script for the show's pilot, Duchovny's manager immediately sent it to his home. After a quick read, Duchovny phoned his manager and told her that he would be happy to meet with the show's producers to discuss the role.

Duchovny attended his first meeting with *The X-Files* production staff wearing a tie with pink pigs on it. Despite his decidedly un-Mulder-like dress sense, Chris Carter was instantly convinced that Duchovny was most definitely the man for the job. Carter was required to present two possible leading men to Fox chiefs, but never doubted that Duchovny would be perfect as Mulder and managed to persuade studio executives to support his choice.

Thus, shortly after his meeting with Carter, Duchovny was presented with a standard five-year contract by Fox. After some careful consideration, Duchovny decided to star in *The X-Files* because 'it had a movie feel about it' and would provide him with 'some good experience and exposure'. When his agent warned him about the commitment involved in joining *The X-Files*, Duchovny admitted that he was convinced that the show would last for

Like Duchovny, Anderson also sensed that the show's strong writing and high production values gave it a 'film-like quality'

'six, maybe 12 episodes at the most' and would never run for five years. Once the series was cancelled, therefore, David figured that he could resume his movie career.

Chris Carter might have found it relatively easy to convince Fox executives to cast Duchovny as Fox Mulder, but he faced an uphill struggle trying to get them to accept or even consider Gillian Anderson in the role of Dana Scully.

The X-Files was just one of many pilot scripts that Anderson read at the beginning of 1993. However, the actress was particularly interested in auditioning for the show because, unlike most television series, it featured a 'strong, independent and intelligent woman as a lead character.' Like David Duchovny, Anderson also sensed that the show's strong writing and high production values gave it a 'film-like quality'.

Unfortunately, when she attended her first audition for the role of Scully, Anderson had absolutely no idea what the character would look like and went along to Randy Stone's office looking extremely scruffy, with her hair half way down her back. However, despite her highly inappropriate appearance, Chris Carter sensed that she would be perfect for the role and declared that she was his first choice as Scully.

During the final stages of casting, it became increasingly clear that Fox executives had their own plans for the role of Scully. While Carter argued the case for Gillian Anderson, Fox executives had always envisaged a glamorous Hollywood supermodel as the show's female lead. In short, they wanted someone more like Pamela Anderson than Gillian Anderson. They also pointed out that Scully was supposed to be 30 years old and Anderson, at 27, was too young for the role (ironically, she was actually only 24 at the time but her agents 'accidentally' gave the Fox network the wrong age) and also far too inexperienced to co-star with Duchovny. Carter just wouldn't compromise and said

that it had to be Anderson. After repeatedly watching Gillian Anderson's total body of television work – an episode of *Class of '96* – Fox eventually relented and decided to try her out in the pilot. Anderson discovered that she had actually won the role a mere two days before filming commenced.

The pilot of *The X-Files* was shot over the course of two weeks in March 1993, on a budget of just over $1 million. As with most of Fox's television productions, it was filmed in and around Vancouver's North Shore Studios in Canada, for economic reasons.

Having grown accustomed to the relatively leisurely pace that films are produced in, David Duchovny was totally shocked by just how arduous *The X-Files* working schedule was. Shooting the pilot took between 14 and 16 hours a day, Monday to Friday, and required its leading actors to be present for most of that time.

Like Duchovny, Gillian Anderson found that the turnaround of a television show was even faster than she had initially expected. 'I desperately needed someone to show me the ropes,' she recalled. 'David did that. He was wonderful.'

Anderson also had problems becoming accustomed to Scully's scientific dialogue. She felt guilty every time she fluffed her lines, especially as Duchovny always seemed to deliver Mulder's jargon with ease.

Upon seeing the first publicity shot of Mulder and Scully together, Anderson was amazed by how much shorter she seemed than her co-star. At 5 feet 3 inches, Gillian is 9 inches shorter than her leading man, although she joked that Scully looked like she only stood up to Mulder's belly button!

Despite such minor difficulties, Duchovny and Anderson developed a strong rapport straight away and became good friends. In fact, some tabloid newspapers claimed that their close friendship developed into a brief romance! However, both denied such reports adamantly. Anderson later admitted that she

Opposite: **Although Duchovny won the role of Fox Mulder with ease, Anderson fought an uphill struggle to convince the studio that she could play Dana Scully**

Above: **The day to day rigours of shooting *The X-Files* were much harder than Duchovny ever expected**

▶▶

found the stories highly amusing and revealed that she loves rumours which have no basis in reality. Duchovny, on the other hand, was deeply offended by the stories and said that he considered all gossip to be unnecessary and harmful.

Whilst shooting the pilot, it became clear that neither Duchovny nor Anderson shared their characters' views on unexplained phenomena. Duchovny revealed that he shared Fox Mulder's emotional detachment and wry sense of humour, but he essentially was a pragmatist and was extremely sceptical about extraterrestrial, supernatural and paranormal forces. He was open to the possibility of their existence, but wouldn't accept it until he is presented with proof.

In subsequent interviews, Duchovny claimed that he only ever experienced the paranormal once – it was a strange sensation called 'love'! He also joked that the only thing that really frightens him is the thought of watching one of his 'lousy' performances.

On a more serious note, the actor revealed that his grandmother told him that she saw the ghost of her late brother, and that he has believed in supernatural forces ever since. 'I have definitely felt the presence of loved ones, though I have never seen anyone,' he said.

He also revealed that he saw an UFO in 1982 whilst studying at Princeton, but doesn't believe that his close encounter proved the existence of extraterrestrial life. Instead, he believed that it was the work of forces closer to home. 'It seemed triangular in shape, somewhat similar to today's stealth bomber,' he explained.

Unlike her co-star, Gillian Anderson has 'always been fascinated' with unexplained phenomena and is not at all like sceptical Dana Scully. The actress considers herself to be 'one of the least straight laced people' in the world and believes in such New Age notions as Extra-Sensory Perception (ESP) and psychokinesis. She has seen psychics for years and keeps *The Tibetan Book of Living and Dying* under her bed. During a vacation in Hawaii, she even spent a lot of time watching the sky looking for UFOs.

Although Scully needed to be convinced about covert governmental activities in *The X-Files*, Anderson has always believed that the public are denied access to a lot of important information by their leaders. She has little doubt that the 1947 Roswell Incident and the accompanying alien autopsy tape are genuine. Anderson also feels that she is probably around a third as intelligent as Scully, but believes that they do share one trait: they're both workaholics.

Scully's least pleasant moment in the pilot of *The X-Files* comes when she has to perform an autopsy on a potential murder victim. Everyone expected that Gillian Anderson would dread filming the scene, but were surprised to learn that she had no qualms whatsoever about working on the sequence. The actress later admitted that part of her has always been 'fascinated by that icky stuff' and that, as a child, she loved dissecting things: she once put a pair of pigs' eyes in a teacher's drawer; and one of her fondest early memories is digging up earthworms in her parents' yard! She also shocked an interviewer who asked her if she could attend a real-life post-mortem by picking up her coat and telling him she was ready to go when he was!

The X-Files pilot received its premiere in front of Fox executives in May 1993. Despite worrying word of mouth before the screening, the assembled audience – which included Fox's owner Rupert Murdoch – reacted positively to the show and actually went as far as to give it a round of applause at the end! A weekly *X-Files* series was commissioned soon after.

Even then, however, Fox researchers did not expect *The X-Files* to be much of a ratings-winner; at best, they hoped the series would attract a loyal audience of intelligent, young professionals aged 18-34, who were always keenly targeted by advertisers. Assuming that the show was destined to fail, Fox scheduled *The X-Files* to air on Fridays at 9pm; a time when most of the potential audience were far away from their televisions, celebrating the start of the weekend in the real world! When Chris Carter asked why his show was placed in such a low-profile and unadventurous timeslot, Fox's Programming Chief told him that *The X-Files* would actually benefit from that position because it meant that the show would be broadcast immediately after the Network's much-touted tongue-in-cheek Western series, *The Adventures of Brisco County, Jr.*, and pick up some of its viewers.

Opposite: **In real life Gillian Anderson would be happy to attend an autopsy**

Above: **Unlike their screen counterparts, Duchovny is sceptical about 'the truth' behind unexplained phenomena while Anderson is a 'true believer'**

▶▶

Both stars made it clear that they were deliberately underplaying the roles to keep the show as believable as possible

Above: Duchovny's canine companion in Vancouver was named 'Blue' after the Bob Dylan song 'Tangled Up In Blue'

Opposite: The actor's fan clubs include 'The David Duchovny Oestrogen Brigade' and 'The Duchovniks'

Carter later learned that the Programming Chief was absolutely convinced that *The Adventures of Brisco County, Jr.* would be a smash hit and had promised to eat his desk if the show's leading man, Bruce Campbell, didn't become a major television star.

Thus, as Duchovny and Anderson travelled to Vancouver to start work on *The X-Files* first season, few held much hope for its future. For Duchovny, life in Vancouver was far more difficult than he expected. He soon started to miss his family, friends and long-time girlfriend, Perrey Reeves, most of whom were a thousand miles away in Los Angeles. As per Perrey's instructions, Duchovny stuck eleven post-it notes on the refrigerator in his new home. Ten of the notes had mind and body guru Deepak Chopra's tips for attaining the fountain of youth inscribed on them. The eleventh simply declared: 'Think about Perrey'. Despite his loneliness, however, Duchovny chose not to spend too much of his free time with his co-star Gillian Anderson, just in case they became sick of each other!

Beside feeling homesick, Duchovny was also a little surprised by how physically and mentally gruelling making *The X-Files* was. Over the course of shooting, he was cut, burned and suffered a serious shoulder injury. Furthermore, he found that it was incredibly difficult to maintain his creativity when required to play the same character 14 hours a day, five or six days a week, for ten months of the year. He initially likened his situation to that of an artist who was ordered to paint all of the time, and concluded that in both cases, the quality of art is diminished.

During the first months of her stay in Vancouver, Gillian Anderson hired a condominium owned by former *21 Jump Street* star Steven Williams. In a strange twist of fate, the actor later returned to Vancouver when he won the role of the sinister Mr. X in the second season of *The X-Files*.

Upon reporting to work, Anderson was required to sacrifice her hair for the good of *The X-Files*. Following the screening of the pilot, Fox executives objected to Scully having shoulder-length hair and so the show's chief hairstylist, Malcolm Marsden, transformed Gillian Anderson's long, wavy, ash-blonde hair into a sleek, strawberry-blonde bob. Apparently, the haircut made Scully look much more professional in the eyes of the studio!

Although Anderson was not as lonely as Duchovny, she also found that it was difficult to adjust to living in Vancouver. Eventually, both stars found friends of the canine variety to keep them company. Anderson bought Cleo, a large, black hound, while Duchovny was offered a fluffy Border collie/terrier to care for after working with her father in an early *X-Files* episode 'Ice'. The actor decided to name his pet 'Blue', after the Bob Dylan song 'Tangled Up in Blue'.

The launch of *The X-Files* proved that even a television phenomenon can have inauspicious beginnings. The show made its debut on September 10th, 1993, to a respectable but unremarkable audience of around seven and a half million. Many critics perceived the show as nothing more than a humourless reworking of *Twin Peaks*, whilst *Entertainment Weekly* wrote, 'the show's a goner'. One of *The X-Files* best reviews came from America's leading listings magazine *TV Guide*, which concluded that the series was 'better than it sounds'. High praise indeed!

Reaction to the show's lead performances was equally mixed. Some critics praised Duchovny and Anderson's beautifully understated portrayals of Mulder and Scully, while other reviewers accused them of practically sleepwalking through the show! However, both stars made it clear that they were deliberately underplaying the roles to keep the show as believable as possible.

'To me, underplaying is reality,' Duchovny told *Cinescape*. 'I've never met anybody who acts like the people on [US super-soap] *Melrose Place*. That's the style of the show. I'm not cutting down the actors. But when we talk about creating realistic characters, we try

– I think both of us try – to react realistically and not dramatically. And that's considered underplaying when you compare and contrast it to the overall style of television acting.'

Anderson told journalists that Chris Carter always wanted Mulder and Scully to be under-played before joking that both she and Duchovny were simply 'too exhausted' to do anything more with the roles!

As *The X-Files* continued to air, David Duchovny sensed that the show wasn't being heavily promoted by the Fox network and was in fact being treated like a poor relative of the network's other new offerings, including *The Adventures of Brisco County Jr.* He was out-raged when he heard that the Network's Programming Chief had promised to eat his desk if Bruce Campbell did not become a superstar and prophetically told him that he would be happy to serve it to the executive later in the year, once *The Adventures of Brisco County Jr.* had bitten the dust.

Despite the show's relative lack of public-ity, *The X-Files* still managed to develop a huge cult following. In much the same way that *Star Trek* fans became known as 'Trekkies' and 'Trekkers', *X-Files* aficionados dubbed themselves 'X-philes' and began to write to the Fox Network as a sign of support for their favourite show.

Furthermore, both David Duchovny and Gillian Anderson became cult figures in their own right. Fans of Fox Mulder's real-life alter-ego formed such groups as 'The David Duchovny Oestrogen Brigade' and 'The Duchovniks'. Besides the usual letters of admiration and autograph requests, the fans inundated their idol with packets of sunflower seeds and ties until Duchovny revealed that, unlike Mulder, he rarely wears ties and doe not chew sunflower seeds all of the time! Duchovny usually laughed off his heartthrob status and simply described his character's appeal as 'an FBI thing'.

On the internet, Anderson's fans discuss such diverse subjects as her eye colour, her preferred breakfast cereal and the best way to start a conversation with Gillian Anderson if you happen to pass her in the street!

Meanwhile, 'The Gillian Anderson Testosterone Brigade', 'Genuine Admirers Of Gillian Anderson', and the less imaginatively titled 'Gillian Anderson Fan Club' were all created as a tribute to the actress behind Dana Scully. On the Internet, Anderson's fans discussed such diverse subjects as her eye colour (blue), her preferred breakfast cereal (muesli and Multi-Grain Cheerios) and the best way to start a conversation with Gillian Anderson if you happen to pass her on the street! Gillian Anderson herself occasionally scanned the fans' databases, but tried not to read them in detail in case anyone's comments had a direct influence on her portrayal of Scully. However, she once admitted that she enjoys reading all the available information the fans have on David Duchovny, and often teases him about it afterwards!

Although it would have been hard to estimate whether Duchovny or Anderson had the largest personal fan following, Duchovny initially dominated all mainstream coverage of *The X-Files*. Despite the fact that he doesn't really like doing interviews and is normally cagey when he does agree to do them, he was clearly considered the star of the show by the press and was constantly asked to grant interviews and attend private photo shoots.

At first, Anderson was upset by the way she was overshadowed by her co-star, but gradually got used to it and started to make a joke of the situation by referring to the actor as the most famous person she knew. 'At first I felt like, "This is our show. It wasn't just his show,"' she later told *Entertainment Weekly*. 'But I learned to not care so much.'

As David Duchovny experienced the full glare of the media spotlight, Gillian Anderson secretly started to date one of *The X-Files* art directors, Clyde Klotz, who joined the show when it became a weekly series. Anderson made the 'first move' by inviting Klotz to her trailer to eat sushi and the pair hit it off straight away. 'We felt like we'd known each other a very long time, and we'd just finally met in person,' the actress subsequently explained to *People* magazine.

During the show's Christmas hiatus, the couple took a holiday in Hawaii. On January 1st, 1994, they decided to tie the knot on the spur of moment. 'It was just the two of us and a Buddhist priest on the 17th hole of the golf course in Hawaii,' Anderson later revealed, 'because that was the most beautiful place we could find on short notice.' They had been dating for just four months at the time.

When they moved into their new home together, Anderson had a strange feeling that someone was literally sitting on her shoulder whenever she walked around the house. She discussed the situation with her husband and a few of her colleagues, one of whom suggested – in true *X-Files* fashion – that she should enlist the help of a Native American Indian to 'cleanse' the house of anything that may still be lingering from the past. Once that was done, Anderson felt much more relaxed and comfortable in the building and never had any strange feelings again!

At the end of *The X-Files* first year, not even the most die-hard X-phile could dispute the fact that the show was in fact a ratings disappointment; it was ranked 113 out of 132 prime-time shows in the US ratings. Normally, such a poor result would have definitely spelt the end of any series.

Upon hearing that Fox had cancelled their cherished Western series *The Adventures Of Brisco County, Jr.*, it seemed highly unlikely that *The X-Files* would be ever be reopened again. However, after carefully considering the show's demographics and foreign sales, Fox decided that they would take a leap of faith with *The X-Files* and commissioned a second season of the show. And that was just the first surprise fate had in store for *The X-Files* cast and crew.

Anderson married *X-Files* art director Clyde Klotz on New Year's Day, 1994, after a whirlwind romance

▶▶

Having narrowly escaped cancellation, *The X-Files* faced a new crisis in the form of Gillian Anderson's pregnancy

During a press conference to mark the launch of the second season of *The X-Files*, David Duchovny laughed when he heard that Fox TV's publicity department had dubbed *The X-Files* as a 'cult hit'. He then told the assembly of journalists that the definition of a cult hit is a series that nobody watches! Little did the actor know that *The X-Files* was about to break the threshold between cult hit and mainstream television phenomenon.

Upon starting work on *The X-Files* second season, the cast and crew had to come to terms with a little-known fact that was destined to soon have a major impact on the show's production: Gillian Anderson was pregnant, and due to give birth on 13th September, 1994 – right in the middle of the year's shooting schedule.

Although the news came as a shock to everyone, including Gillian Anderson, the actress had already received a strange omen of the future in the winter of 1993, at an *X-Files* publicity event held by Fox in Burbank, California. During a break in proceedings, Anderson consulted a psychic, Debi Becker, who told her, 'You're going to have a little girl.' At that time, Anderson dismissed the prediction and told Becker that her work on *The X-Files* precluded her from finding the time to even think about having a baby. However, the actress' attitude changed dramatically at the beginning of February when she realised she was pregnant, as a result of her whirlwind marriage to Clyde Klotz.

David Duchovny was the first of Gillian's colleagues to learn about her condition. The actress told him during the final days of shooting the show's first season and he immediately asked her if she was happy about the news. When Anderson said she was, Duchovny offered his congratulations and promised to keep the pregnancy a secret.

After putting it off for as long as she could, Anderson eventually got round to telling the producers about her shocking discovery. During their conversation, she could immediately sense that she could be in danger of losing her role on the series.

'I was ready for anything at that point,' Anderson later revealed. 'I was making a huge life decision and it was more about the decision that I was making for myself than the decision I was making for them. I really would have rolled with whatever punches that they would have given me. It would have been unfortunate and sad to not do the show but if that was how they reacted and it meant spending more time with my child then that wasn't such a bad thing.'

Thus, *The X-Files* writing staff were faced with an incredibly difficult dilemma: how could they explain the fact that a single and unattached woman like Dana Scully was pregnant? While they struggled to come up with a plausible answer, Fox studio chiefs were informed of the news and immediately suggested that Dana Scully should be re-cast, killed off or replaced by another female agent. They were reportedly furious that Anderson would let her private life jeopardise the show and felt that it would be easier in the long term just to drop her.

As a result, series creator/executive producer Chris Carter once again found himself out on a limb as he argued the case for keeping Anderson in the show. Carter was keen to protect the relationship he had built between Mulder and Scully, and felt that the show's quality and popularity would be undermined if one of the characters was removed from the show. Eventually, after exploring all possible options, a compromise was reached.

Opposite: The beloved Mulder/Scully partnership was jeopardised by Gillian Anderson's pregnancy

Above: After a great deal of debate, the producers decided not to write her out of the series

▶▶

'After I had Piper, I became more positive, more open, more caring'

Gillian Anderson gave birth to her daughter, Piper Maru, on September 25th, 1994. A mere ten days later, she back at work on the set of *The X-Files*

It was decided that Anderson's pregnancy would not be written into the series. The FBI's X-Files division, which had been temporarily shut down at the end of the show's first year, would remain closed in order to keep Mulder and Scully separated from each other. Whilst Mulder pursued his investigations as energetically as ever, Scully would co-ordinate operations from the comfort of her own office and offer the occasional piece of advice and information via her trusty telephone. In that way, Anderson could endure her pregnancy and still be a part of *The X-Files*. To make her life even more bearable, the show's shooting schedule was suited around the actress; she was usually required to work for three of the eight days of filming and was then allowed to take time off.

In order to hide the 52 pounds Anderson gained during her pregnancy, Dana Scully suddenly developed a penchant for lose-fitting suits – suits which became baggier with every episode. The actress was also filmed exclusively from the shoulders up, and a stand-in was hired to play Scully for full-length, long shots.

The writing staff, camera crew and costume designers did a tremendous job of keeping Anderson's pregnancy a secret; if you didn't know about it, you probably wouldn't have suspected anything. However, eagle-eyed X-philes noticed that Anderson almost gave the game away in an episode called 'The Host'; in the scene where Scully meets Mulder and sits down next to him on a park bench, Anderson's condition is clear for all to see!

On 23rd September, Anderson temporarily left the series on maternity leave. To explain her absence, Dana Scully was abducted by unknown forces in the episode, 'Duane Barry'. Although it initially looked to be the work of aliens, the event was shrouded in mystery and became a part of *The X-Files* myths. Once 'Duane Barry' completed filming, Anderson shot a few brief dream sequences for the next instalment, 'Ascension', in which Mulder searched for his missing partner. For the scene in which he imagines that Scully is being experimented upon by aliens, Anderson displayed her pregnant stomach!

Two days after her departure, the actress gave birth to a baby girl, Piper Maru Anderson, via Caesarean Section. Piper weighed 8lb, 10oz. Both mother and daughter were inundated by gifts from loyal 'X-philes' at the hospital, their Vancouver home and at *The X-Files* production office. Gillian was stunned by the amount of gifts, flowers and messages she received and later sent thank-you messages via her assistant to as many of her fans as she could. As a tribute to Chris Carter's continued support, Gillian asked him to be her daughter's godfather. He was more than happy to accept and later named an episode of *The X-Files* 'Piper Maru' after her.

As far as Gillian Anderson was concerned, motherhood was a life-altering experience. 'After I had Piper, I became more positive, more open, more caring,' she said. 'I think I've become a better person.'

After spending six days in hospital, Anderson went home to recuperate. For the only time in her life, she watched television incessantly. Among other things, the actress saw her very first episode of the most successful cult TV show of all time, *Star Trek*, and thought that it was 'one of the most fabulous things in the world'.

With Scully missing , David Duchovny was left on his own to investigate *The X-Files* for two episodes. Although Anderson featured briefly in 'Ascension', it was essentially a showcase for Duchovny who seized the opportunity to perform some of the show's most ambitious stunt scenes, including a cable car chase worthy of James Bond.

The following instalment, entitled '3', was the only episode of the series that completely lacked the presence Dana Scully. At the behest of Fox executives, the episode also matched Mulder with another female lead, to see if *The X-Files* worked without the famous Mulder-Scully pairing. '3' guest-starred Duchovny's real-life girlfriend, Perrey Reeves, as a member of a sinister cult group who becomes a prime suspect in a series of

'We would have not been that creative had Gillian not been pregnant'

The X-Files surprise win for Best Dramatic Series at the 1995 Golden Globe Awards gave the show's ratings a welcome boost

vampire murders. During the course of the episode, Perrey's character embarks on a brief affair with Mulder.

Luckily for Anderson, '3' was not one of the most popular episodes of *The X-Files*. Most viewers complained that they missed Dana Scully, while Duchovny himself said that the episode lacked logic and found it unbelievable that the typically-chaste Mulder suddenly became involved with a blood-sucking murder suspect!

X-philes demanding the return of Gillian Anderson didn't have to wait long. A mere ten days after she gave birth, the actress was ordered back in front of the cameras for the episode 'One Breath', in which Scully is mysteriously found in a Washington hospital, where she recovers from a coma. Despite the fact that Scully spent most of the episode lying down in her hospital bed, it was still difficult for Anderson to get used to working again so quickly after giving birth. She felt 'exhausted, sore, emotional and pissed off' during the making of the show, and actually fell asleep when one of Scully's coma scenes was being shot!

Life became even harder for the actress in the following episode, 'Firewalker'. A standard *X-Files* adventure, 'Firewalker' entailed a lot of running and jumping for Mulder and Scully. 'It was physically difficult, and emotionally – well, I shed a lot of silent tears,' Anderson told Canada's *Woman Magazine*. 'It was horrible. There were plenty of times that all I wanted to do was quit and be with my baby. But then I would have had a lawsuit on my hands, for breach of contract.'

Slowly but surely, Anderson regained her strength and became accustomed to the trials and tribulations of filming *The X-Files* once again. Just as she reached full strength, however, the actress was horrified to learn that she would be required to put a live cricket in her mouth for the episode, 'Humbug'. When it came to filming that scene, Gillian tried to not to think about it and got it over with as quickly as possible. Some tabloids later claimed that she actually swallowed the cricket, but the

actress was quick to establish the truth behind the incident. 'I didn't even taste it,' she explained. 'It was just kind of wriggling around in my mouth, and then I spat it out.'

The second season of *The X-Files* premiered on 16th September 1994, by which time Anderson's pregnancy was public knowledge. 'X-philes' speculated about how her condition would be explained in the series, and rumours started to circulate that she would be kidnapped and impregnated by aliens. Although this was clearly wide of the mark, it helped generate interest in the show and its first episode was watched by just under ten million viewers in the USA alone.

The majority of *The X-Files* cast and crew also believed that Anderson's pregnancy actually benefited the show on an artistic level. As Duchovny told *Sci-Fi Universe Magazine*: 'We would not have been that creative had Gillian not been pregnant.'

The first sign that *The X-Files* was moving into the mainstream came when its stars were invited to visit the FBI Headquarters in Washington. During their tour of the building, it soon became apparent to Duchovny and Anderson that the couple have a lots of fans in the organisation. Despite their popularity, however, both were accompanied by FBI agents at all times (even when they went to the bathroom!) and were told in no uncertain terms that there were no such things as real-life X-Files in their organisation.

The X-Files really took off at the beginning of 1995, when the show won the prestigious Golden Globe Award for Best Dramatic Series, beating the likes of *ER* and *NYPD Blue*. The prize was collected by Chris Carter, Anderson and Duchovny, none of whom expected to win. In fact, they were so shocked to hear the announcement that they initially thought it was a mistake and didn't leave their table to collect the prize!

That wasn't the only surprise the Golden Globe Awards had in store for the *X-Files* crew. The first one came near the beginning of the event when celebrated American singer Tony Bennett walked up to Duchovny and

Carter to tell them how much he enjoyed *The X-Files*. Later in the evening, Gillian Anderson started talking to cult filmmaker Quentin Tarantino, who she assumed would know who she was and would also be a bit of an X-phile. Unfortunately, she was wrong. 'He was polite, but he had no idea who I was,' the actress laughed afterwards.

The new-found popularity of *The X-Files* was consolidated by a series of further accolades, including the Saturn Award, a Parent's Choice prize and The Environmental Media Award. At the influential Viewers For Quality Television (VQT) Awards, *The X-Files* was nominated for best drama series while Duchovny and Anderson both won nominations for their performances as Fox Mulder and Dana Scully.

By the Spring of 1995, Duchovny and Anderson had started to consider *The X-Files'* growing success. Duchovny suggested that the show's appeal lay in its spiritualism and its believable conspiracy theories. He concluded that either the show was 'tapping into something people want' or that 'the Fox Network has an amazing marketing department.'

Anderson decided that X-philes tuned into the show each week because they want escapist fun. 'What makes it a hit is the fact that it allows people to escape to another world, another reality far removed from their own, for a little while,' she said.

Another aspect of the show which had caught viewers' imagination was the relationship between Mulder and Scully. Although Chris Carter avoided suggesting a romantic attraction between the two FBI agents in early episodes, he accepted that their relationship had taken on a will-they/won't-they slant worthy of *Moonlighting*, *The Avengers* and *Remmington Steele*. Consequently, both of the show's stars were constantly asked whether or not the two characters would be involved with each other in a future episode.

Duchovny felt that *The X-Files* was one of the few projects which allowed him to play a character who was not 'sexually-orientated'. Having portrayed countless boyfriends, rakes and a cross-dressing FBI agent, the actor enjoyed the idea that Mulder was dedicated to his mission to find 'The Truth'. As a result, he has no desire to see Mulder embarking on a romantic relationship with anyone. The actor

During the show's second season, David Duchovny started to develop storylines for several episodes. By the end of _The X-Files_ second year, Anderson and Duchovny had become household names

is adamant that _The X-Files_ isn't about Mulder and Scully's private lives and feels that the show would be undermined by any such changes to its format.

Anderson admits that both she and Duchovny try to 'play up' the mutual attraction between the two agents as much as they can. 'Whenever we're acting together – it's there,' she said. However, she shares her co-star's view that an affair would not benefit the show and believes that 'Mulder and Scully should save their passion for their work.' Towards the end of shooting the show's second season, Duchovny decided that he would become actively involved with the creation and development of storylines. Duchovny, a longtime admirer of actor/playwright Sam Shepard, already made a substantial input into the of the show (Anderson once said that 'he goes over scripts like an English teacher') and came up with an idea for an episode whilst reading an article in _New Yorker_ magazine concerning the 'racial purity' policies of General Franco. The actor pitched a tale of extraterrestrial breeding and cloning to Chris Carter, who subsequently developed the idea to form an epic two-part adventure, 'Colony', and 'End Game'. Carter also wrote the screenplays for the episodes when Duchovny said that that he simply wouldn't have the time to do it himself due to his filming commitments on the show.

'Colony' and 'End Game' proved to be two of most popular _X-Files_ episodes of the year. Flushed with his initial success, Duchovny contributed another story idea. Chris Carter transformed the premise into the show's cliffhanging second season finale, 'Anasazi', in which Mulder gained access to a computer disc containing 'The Truth'.

Besides being his second foray into writing for _The X-Files_, 'Anasazi', also marked David Duchovny's debut as a stunt co-ordinator. Whilst waiting for the show's regular stunt co-ordinator to choreograph a fight scene between Mulder and the sinister FBI Agent Krycek (Nicholas Lea), the actors gradually grew impatient and eventually decided to plan the fight themselves. They deliberately tried to avoid staging a 'typical TV fight' and instead filmed a 'dirty and tough' struggle for survival.

By the end of the show's second year, few could deny that _The X-Files_ was a critical and commercial smash hit. In the USA alone, it had

a loyal audience of more than 10 million, which was nothing short of incredible given its timeslot. _The X-Files_ was instantly renewed by Fox, whilst the series which aired beforehand (the sci-fi adventure shows _M.A.N.T.I.S._ and _VR.5_) were both cancelled.

As a result, Duchovny and Anderson swiftly became household names. Although Duchovny was a minor celebrity when he started work on _The X-Files_, he was unprepared for international stardom. Over the course of a few months, Duchovny decided that fame was simply 'no fun' and grew sick and tired of people shouting 'Hi Mulder!' to

him on the street. Eventually, he started to reply 'My name's David, okay!' In an ideal world, Duchovny would prefer to be famous for something else – like curing a disease or writing a great book – than for his work as an actor. However, he accepts that fame 'comes with the territory' and tries to be polite and friendly to X-philes providing they respect his privacy and, of course, don't call him Mulder!

To make matters worse, Duchovny not only had to cope with his new-found fame but also had to come to terms with the break-up of his three year old relationship with Perrey Reeves. The actor said that they could no

longer handle being 1,000 miles apart for 10 months a year. 'I guess you can call our relationship a casualty of The X-Files,' he said.

Unlike Duchovny, Gillian Anderson was a virtual unknown prior to her assignment to The X-Files. At first, she felt awkward about her new-found fame. 'It's strange when you hear your personal name called and you turn around expecting to see somebody you know and you're face-to-face with a complete stranger,' she said. 'But it's very flattering and everyone's so positive about the show.'

The actress subsequently learned to cope with her celebrity status, but revealed that it is

During the second season hiatus, Anderson embarked on a publicity tour of Europe where she enjoyed virtual anonymity. David Duchovny began to break away from his public image as Fox Mulder by hosting *Saturday Night Live* and appearing in *The Larry Sanders Show*

a headache whenever she tries to spend some time alone with her husband and child. Once work on the second season of *The X-Files* was completed, Anderson agreed to participate in a European publicity tour and loved the anonymity she and her family experienced in London, Milan and Paris.

While his co-star explored Europe, Duchovny gave two performances that challenged the public's perception of his range and talent. The first came in the popular US comedy series *Saturday Night Live*. Duchovny convinced the show's producers that he would be able to host an episode of the series during a friendly basketball match and, despite being extremely nervous, had 'a lot of fun' filming his appearance. The actor started the show in drag as a homage to his role as Dennis/Denise Bryson in *Twin Peaks* and went on to play Batman's assistant Robin before ending proceedings as himself. He had planned to mimic the show's main guest, Rod Stewart, but was told not to at the last minute by the producers in case he caused offence. Nevertheless, Duchovny's stint of *Saturday Night Live* was considered a huge success and the actor was proud of the end result.

The actor was equally pleased with his work as a guest star on his favourite television series, *The Larry Sanders Show*. When he discussed the possibility of appearing on the spoof chat show with its producers, Duchovny's only condition was that he could play himself as a 'real jerk' and be rude to the eponymous Mr. Sanders (played by Garry Shandling). Upon hearing his demand, Shandling warned the actor not to appear unlikable in case it harmed his public image. It was then that Duchovny assured Shandling that he wasn't bothered what people thought of him and told him that he really wanted to show a different side of himself to the character people had grown accustomed to in *The X-Files*. Shandling relented and the actor was as rude and obnoxious as only the most spoiled Hollywood star could be!

After months of procrastination, David finally agreed to his first session on an *X-Files* computer bulletin board. The actor chatted to around 100 X-philes across cyberspace, but found that it was something of a disappointing experience. He enjoyed answering their questions, but found that he spent most of his time saying 'hello' and 'goodbye' to 100 people, which he understandably felt was rather pointless. He was subsequently amused to hear that one of the fans who participated in the discussion added an essential fact to his *X-Files* database immediately afterwards – 'David Duchovny likes saying "hello" and "goodbye" a lot'!

Duchovny subsequently scanned the Internet for Worldwide Web sites dedicated to *The X-Files* and was surprised by the level of detail fans discuss the show in. For example, he read a message from one fan who couldn't understand why Scully was able to jump into Mulder's car and drive off in it without readjusting the car's seat or mirrors!

The actor was similarly surprised to learn about the amount of interest that his appearance in a small pair of red Speedo swimming trunks in one episode of the series had generated. In this case, however, Duchovny soon saw the funny side of the situation and later told fans that he was going to either put the trunks on auction or donate them to the Smithsonian Institute, where they can hang alongside other pieces of television memorabilia!

Duchovny's celebrity status earned him an invitation to attend the star-studded premiere of *Batman Forever*. Prior to attending, he was simply looking forward to seeing the film free of charge and consequently was not prepared for the media circus surrounding the event. He was taken aback by the barrage of questions he faced, which ranged from 'Are you looking forward to seeing the movie?' to 'Who made your suit?' and 'What would you do to help Clinton get the Health Care Plan passed'?

Following his experience at the premiere, Duchovny decided that he would probably enjoy events more if he went to them as a paying member of the general public. Thus, he was spotted in the audience at a Rolling Stones' concert, which he attended to see his favourite musician, Keith Richards.

Similarly, when Gillian Anderson attended a concert given by Quintron, she was recognised by someone near her in the crowd. The young man went up to her and told that she really looked like 'the woman from *The X-Files*'. The actress simply thanked him for the compliment!

6/America's Most Wanted

By 1996, *The X-Files* had made the transition from cult hit to television phenomenon

Top: David Duchovny meets another famous X-phile, *Happy Days* star Henry Winkler

Above: Gillian Anderson comes face to face with her fans during her first *X-Files* convention

As the cast and crew of *The X-Files* worked on its third season, the show's popularity was never in doubt. Besides being a surprise success in the American ratings, *The X-Files* was a smash hit in more than 60 countries and was the most-watched television series in Japan and Spain. The show continued to win rave reviews and was nominated for a staggering six Emmy Awards, including those for Best Drama Series, Best Writing and Best Cinematography. *X-Files* merchandising spin-offs, such as books, T-Shirts, mugs and baseball caps, helped develop the cultural phenomenon and proved extremely lucrative for the Fox corporation.

Inevitably, the show's worldwide popularity fuelled the public's growing interest in unsolved mysteries and unexplained phenomena, and also contributed to a substantial rise in reported UFO sightings. A number of television shows, magazines and books devoted to exploring real-life strange phenomena helped feed the public's new-found curiosity with the unexplained.

Thus, *The X-Files* almost single-handedly allowed science fiction to shed its unfashionable image and made it the most provocative and lucrative genre of the Nineties. Dubbed the 'hippest show on Earth' by some critics, *The X-Files* converted virtually everyone in Hollywood to its cause. Prolific writers such as Cyberpunk guru William Gibson, renowned sci-fi author Harlan Ellison and the legendary horror scribe Stephen King all agreed to provide scripts for future episodes of the series. *The X-Files* album, 'Songs In The Key of X – Music Inspired By *The X-Files*' attracted the likes of Sheryl Crow, REM, Brian Eno, Foo Fighters, Danzig and Filter. Famous X-philes included Steven Spielberg, Winona Ryder, Bruce Springsteen, Whoopi Goldberg, Martin Short, Jonathan Ross and Robin Williams.

Whilst relaxing on the set of *The X-Files*, a production assistant told David Duchovny that Robin Williams wanted to meet him.

Duchovny said that he didn't believe him – and then was embarrassed to learn that Williams was standing at the other side of the set! Duchovny felt honoured that an actor of Williams' stature took the time to visit him, but generally isn't much of a star-spotter. 'It is more satisfying to me to deal with the people who tried to help me a long time ago, who believed in me, who told me to just hang in there,' he explained.

Some of the show's most famous fans, especially Whoopi Goldberg and Martin Short, lobbied tirelessly for guest roles in the series. However, Duchovny was opposed to the idea of using celebrity guest stars on the show because he felt that it would undermine the show's realism. 'A lot of the show's power comes from it being believable,' he said. 'So it's hard to cast recognisable people – it just takes you right out of it.'

Chris Carter's mission for *The X-Files* third season was to consolidate the show's success whilst trying to keep the audience on the edge of their seats. He also attempted to give Dana Scully a bigger role in the proceedings. Carter considered the *X-Files* stars as a double act of equal proportion and was aware that Gillian Anderson had complained about her character's lot during the show's first two years.

▶▶

'I'm not good at smart, witty, two-line comments that can't be misinterpreted'

Top: Once overshadowed by her co-star, Anderson received more screen time and media attention during the *X Files* third season

Above: Anderson was shocked to win the Screen Actors' Guild Award for Best Actress

'I think she's been chasing in Mulder's footsteps for long enough,' the actress stated prior to the start of season three. 'They've certainly written her as being competent enough to do the investigations and it gets tiring to always be one step behind. At first, it made sense in the flow of the show and the way the show was set up and the way Scully wasn't supposed to have witnessed very much, but I think that now she has, it's time to move forward with her.'

Chris Carter might have regarded Duchovny and Anderson as stars of equal magnitude, but the Fox network clearly saw things differently. Prior to the start of *The X-Files* third season, David Duchovny received a substantial pay raise as a tribute to his contribution to the show's remarkable success and his solo reign in Anderson's absence; most reports claim that his salary increased from $35,000 to $100,000 per episode! Clearly, therefore, Fox regarded Duchovny as the show's main asset.

To her credit, Gillian Anderson refused to criticise Fox for its decision. Whenever she was asked about her feelings on Duchovny's massive wage increase, she would simply point out that actresses have always been paid less than actors and would then simply change the subject.

Thus, it was business as usual for Anderson during the show's third year. She would always take Piper to the set and her nanny would care for her when her mother was required in front of the cameras. Although *The X-Files* is famous for scaring viewers on a regular basis, Piper was rarely surprised or upset by anything she saw on the show's set; ironically, the only thing that frightened her was a sinister Santa Claus who appeared in one episode of the show. When Piper lost her front tooth, she could be seen on and around the set clutching an alien doll. The doll wore a T-shirt declaring the immortal words: 'The tooth is out there'!

The X-Files third season made its debut on September 22nd, 1995, amidst a massive wave of publicity. Judging by the amount of

attention the show's return received, it was clear that *The X-Files* had caught the public's imagination and easily stood alongside America's leading programmes, *Friends*, *ER*, *Frasier* and *NYPD Blue*.

In January 1996, Gillian Anderson attended her first *X-Files* convention in Burbank, California, together with Chris Carter. Duchovny had also been invited but decided to decline the offer, on the grounds that he was just an actor and anything he said about *The X-Files* was superfluous; he felt that the only thing that really mattered was his performance in the show. Prior to the event, Anderson was extremely apprehensive about what to expect and was particularly worried by the prospect of meeting the show's most fervent fans, who she feared were going to be 'really strange'. A few days before, she told *The LA Times* that she had decided that it would definitely be her 'first and last' convention appearance.

Upon entering the convention's auditorium, Anderson was overwhelmed by the enthusiastic reception she received from the fans. In fact, she was so startled that she chose not to give the opening speech she had prepared for the event and immediately started to answer questions from the crowd. Ironically, one of the first enquiries she faced concerned why David Duchovny received more media coverage and money than she did. Anderson was clearly more than a little surprised that a fan would ask her such a business-orientated question, but she quickly regained her composure and replied, 'Maybe it's my time now.'

Besides the inevitable questions about the much-touted Mulder/Scully romance, Anderson was frequently asked how Scully could remain a sceptic after she had confronted so many extraordinary forces and quite possibly been kidnapped by aliens! The actress calmly explained that Scully 'automatically goes back to science before she can jump to any philosophical conclusions.'

Despite her fears, Anderson later described the convention as a 'wonderful experience,' and hinted that she might appear at other such events in the future.

A week after the Burbank *X-Files* convention, David Duchovny and Gillian Anderson attended the Golden Globe Award ceremony. They had been nominated for best actor and actress respectively, but sadly the prizes were collected by *NYPD Blue* star Dennis Franz and Jane Seymour for her work as *Dr Quinn, Medicine Woman*. Oddly, *The X-Files* was not even nominated as best drama series, even though it had actually won the award the previous year!

On February 24th, Gillian Anderson won the Screen Actors' Guild of America award for Best Actress. Anderson was clearly stunned and had be coaxed to collect her prize by her co-star David Duchovny, who had been nominated for the best actor prize claimed by Anthony Edwards of *ER* fame.

Upon receiving her award, it became clear that Anderson hadn't even thought of preparing a thank-you speech. She opened her address by stating that she had 'absolutely nothing to say' and then admitted that she 'didn't expect this at all.' The actress then thanked David Duchovny, her husband Clyde Klotz, her daughter Piper, Chris Carter and *X-Files* writers/producers James Wong and Glen Morgan – before remembering Wong and Morgan had left *The X-Files* at the beginning of its second year to work on their own series, *Space: Above and Beyond!*

Back on the set, Duchovny contributed two further story ideas for *The X-Files*. The first, 'Avatar', focused on the show's principal supporting character, Mulder and Scully's boss Walter Skinner (Mitch Pileggi) and the screenplay was written by the series' co-executive producer, Howard Gordon. The second episode, 'Talitha Cumi', was developed by Chris Carter into the year's cliff-hanging finale and pitted Mulder and Scully against a shape-shifting alien.

Never one to sit on his laurels, Duchovny continued to branch out by appearing in a wide range of unusual projects. The actor provided a guest voice in the cult animated series *Duckman* and also joined a great tradition of celebrity callers in *Frasier*. As a personal favour to former *X-Files* writer/producers Glen Morgan and James Wong, Duchovny guest-starred as an android pool shark, 'Handsome Alvin' in an episode of *Space: Above And Beyond* entitled 'R & R'. His appearance won an increase in ratings, but wasn't enough to save the show from cancellation.

Both Duchovny and Anderson performed vocal duties for an instalment of Fox's other television sensation, *The Simpsons*. In an episode entitled 'The Springfield File', they play – yes, you guessed it! – a pair of FBI agents who are sent to Springfield to investigate Homer Simpson's UFO sightings.

Anderson also worked as a voice artist on *Reboot*, the popular computer-animated series on which her husband Clyde Klotz served as an artist. In her episode of the show, the actress played a character who was strongly reminiscent of Dana Scully. David Duchovny was due to join her in the recording studio to voice her partner, but couldn't find the time to fit it into his busy schedule.

During the early part of 1996, David Duchovny started to date actress Dana Wheeler-Nicholson. The former fiancee of rock legend Eric Clapton, Dana met Duchovny whilst starring in *The X-Files* episode 'Syzygy' and they began a romantic relationship shortly after.

It was around the same time that Gillian Anderson found herself in hot water over an interview she gave to the *Los Angeles Times*. During the interview, she had described *The X-Files* shooting schedule as 'a death sentence'. Although Anderson later stated that her comment was nothing more than 'a meaningless joke', Chris Carter called her immediately after reading the interview and told her that *The X-Files* represented 'a chance of a lifetime' and that everyone's hard work would all be worthwhile in the end. Anderson promised him that she would never be so careless again.

In a subsequent interview for the magazine *Entertainment Weekly*, Gillian Anderson

David Duchovny started dating actress Dana Wheeler-Nicholson after she guest-starred in the *X-Files* episode 'Syzygy'

▶▶

'When the world blows up, I don't think anyone is going to care that there were three missing episodes of the *X-Files*'

Above: **Duchovny has persuaded the producers of *The X-Files* to cut short the number of episodes filmed, so that he can pursue other screen roles**

Opposite: **As the host of *Future Fantastic* Gillian Anderson explored the thin line between science fiction and science fact**

suggested that she was too honest and not witty enough in interviews. 'I'm not good at smart, witty, two-line comments that can't be misinterpreted,' she said. She also joked that it always takes her half an hour to decipher one paragraph of any interview with her academic co-star, David Duchovny!

In April, *The X-Files* won the People's Choice Award at the BAFTAs in recognition of the show's international popularity. Chris Carter, David Duchovny and Gillian Anderson accepted the prize via satellite.

Despite their success and popularity, however, shooting *The X-Files* was as hard as ever. David Duchovny was required to co-star with as many as 300 cockroaches in the episode, 'War of the Coprophages'! Gillian Anderson, meanwhile, learned that she had to fight a crazy cat in 'Teso Dos Bichos' – a task made more difficult because she is allergic to felines! After a lot of careful consideration, the show's special effects crew made a dummy of the cat which was actually covered in rabbit fur. Anderson then spent three hours fighting with the doll.

'It was the stupidest thing I've ever done' she laughed afterwards. 'It was take after take of fighting and rolling around with this bunny-covered cat on my face. The fur was coming off, going up my nose, and sticking to my lipstick. That was the worst!'

Towards the end of shooting the show's third season, David Duchovny started to admit that he was very worried about being typecast. 'I want to make more movies,' he stated. 'I don't want to be known as Mulder for the rest of my life.'

Consequently, in a pre-emptive strike against the threat of typecasting, Duchovny convinced *The X-Files* producers to cut production of the show's third season from 25 to 24 episodes, and the fourth season was reduced from 25 episodes to 22. This would allow the actor to pursue more film projects during the hiatus. As soon as the show's fans started to express their dismay at his decision, Duchovny put things into context. 'When the

world blows up, I don't think anyone is going to care that there were three missing episodes of *The X-Files*', he quipped.

In a bid to keep the show's fans happy, Duchovny agreed to star with Gillian Anderson in *The X-Files* CD-ROM game. The pair shot live-action footage which was then incorporated into the computerised adventure. In this way, the general public were given the opportunity to play Mulder and Scully!

Once he had fulfilled his filming commitments on *The X-Files*, David Duchovny immediately started work on his first film in three years, *Playing God*. Directed by Andy Wilson, *Playing God* stars Duchovny as a drug-addicted surgeon who loses his licence and is recruited by the mob to operate on underworld figures. Timothy Hutton and Angelina Jolie lead the film's supporting cast.

Duchovny also discussed a number of projects which he could work on in the summer of 1997 and became particularly interested in playing the lead role in *Permanent Midnight*. Based on the real-life story of script writer Jerry Stahl, *Permanent Midnight* is believed to follow his descent into drink and drug abuse while he worked on such series as *Moonlighting* and, ironically, *Twin Peaks*.

As Duchovny pursued movie stardom at top gear, Gillian Anderson chose a different path. Although her agent had been inundated with film and television projects to consider, Anderson felt that none of the roles on offer were suitable for her. Instead, she agreed to narrate two documentaries, *Spies Above Us* and *Why Planes Go Down*, and recorded a best-selling audio adaptation of Kevin J. Anderson's *X-Files* novel *Ground Zero*.

Gillian Anderson also started work as the host of BBC TV's glossy documentary series, *Future Fantastic*. Produced by the team behind *Tomorrow's World*, *Future Fantastic* explores the increasingly close relationship between science fiction and science fact. The series also celebrates the scientific achievements of the last hundred years, and predicts life in 21st century.

Many Hollywood insiders were surprised that the *X-Files* star was happy to work in science fiction again and wondered if she was in danger of being typecast as a result. However, Anderson was quick to explain why she decided to host the show.

'When I first started doing *The X-Files*, I was inundated by requests to do anything and everything to do with sci-fi and the paranormal, but I turned it all down', she said. 'But *Future Fantastic* is different – it's being done from a comprehensive, intelligent perspective which just seems right.'

During the nine-part series, Anderson examined virtually every aspect of science fiction and science fact, from nano-technology to the intricacies of time travel. Of all the futuristic hardware featured in the show, the actress was most interested in the teleporter, which she hoped would become a reality because it would allow her to travel across the world in seconds. She also liked the idea of owning the world's first invisible suit, because she could use it to 'get up to lots of mischievous things!'

Once her summer assignments were completed, Anderson and family visited Australia on an *X-Files* promotional tour. As part of her travels, the actress visited a shopping centre in Melbourne and was amazed to find no less than 10,000 people waiting for her! In short, Gillian Anderson received a reception worthy of The Beatles.

'I've not experienced anything like it,' Gillian Anderson said afterwards. 'I've never made a mall appearance before, so I really had no point of reference. When I did the convention in the States we had 3,000, but that was all the place could hold. The welcome [in Melbourne] had been overwhelming; absolutely incredible.'

Back in America, Anderson accepted an invitation to host an episode of the real-life crime show, *America's Most Wanted*. Judging by events in Melbourne, that description could easily be applied to David Duchovny and Gillian Anderson.

7/Life after X

Once *The X-Files* ceases production, Anderson and Duchovny will have to overcome the problem of typecasting

Above: David Duchovny would end *The X-Files* television series with a romance between Mulder and Scully

Opposite: Gillian Anderson might have less trouble escaping typecasting than her high profile co-star

I n the space of just three years, *The X-Files* has emerged as a bona fide television and cultural phenomenon. A critical and commercial smash hit, the show continues to win new viewers across the globe and shows no sign of losing any of its sudden popularity.

Despite its remarkable success, however, it is extremely unlikely that the series will last beyond 1998. Once their original five-year contracts expire, David Duchovny and Gillian Anderson will be keen to escape from *The X-Files* gruelling production schedule and will probably seize the opportunity to play different roles in a wide range of projects.

Of course, the end of the weekly *X-Files* series almost certainly won't spell the end of FBI Special Agents Fox Mulder and Dana Scully's extraordinary adventures. *The X-Files* is set to continue in the form of movies which are could emulate the success of *Star Trek's* big screen outings. Fox TV might also launch a spin-off series from *The X-Files* (jokily dubbed as 'The Y-Files' by some reporters) in which a set of new characters would pursue Mulder and Scully's investigations.

David Duchovny never expected *The X-Files* to last more than six to twelve episodes, let alone penetrate popular culture. 'I'm truly amazed at our success', he stated. 'After all, when it comes down to it, it's just a TV series.'

The actor considers himself very lucky to be part of a successful, high-quality television show, but admits that working in television was never one of his goals. Instead, he always imagined himself 'hopping from one glorious movie to another.'

During the course of *The X-Files* three-year history, Duchovny has been repeatedly invited to play a larger role in the production of the show. He has contributed several story ideas and plans to write and direct a few episodes of the series before its end. While Duchovny appreciates all the opportunities the producers have presented him, he is well aware that their main motive is to keep him happy with his role in the show. 'It reminds me of playing with my dog,' he told *Time Out*. 'I'll give him a choice between a tennis ball or a frisbee – whatever it takes to keep him involved.'

As far as *The X-Files* are concerned, Duchovny's burning ambition is to play basketball in an episode of the show. The actor previously managed to demonstrate his basketball skills in *The Red Shoe Diaries* and hopes that the writers of *The X-Files* will incorporate them into Mulder's character. 'Mandy Patinkin got to sing falsetto every week on *Chicago Hope*,' said Duchovny. 'I don't see why we can't do something that plays to my strengths.'

Despite constant rumours to the contrary, however, Duchovny has no intention of reprising his role as cross-dressing FBI agent Dennis/Denise Bryson in an *X-Files*/Twin Peaks crossover episode. Although *Twin Peaks* creator David Lynch has expressed his fondness for *The X-Files*, Chris Carter has publicly stated that such a crossover will never happen.

When *The X-Files* ceases production as a weekly series, Duchovny would give fans what they want: he would end the show with

▶▶

Life After X

Top: **When *The X-Files* leaves our TV screens, Duchovny will pursue movie stardom as well as try his hand at writing and directing. Anderson, meanwhile, will continue to act and devote more of her time to charity work**

Above: **Following her co-star's lead, Anderson has started to redefine her public image**

Mulder and Scully finally embarking on a romantic relationship together. Assuming an *X-Files* movie is to follow, he would then bring the dynamic duo face to face with the extra-terrestrials they have been hunting for so long because 'It will be interesting to see how we react when we can actually see an alien or two.'

Duchovny believes that he could play Fox Mulder until his 45th birthday, by which time he would have to bow out and find a 'serious job'! He appreciates that the huge success of *The X-Files* threatens to typecast him as Mulder, but has already started to take pre-ventative measures against that danger. The actor intends to pursue his movie career full-time once *The X-Files* is behind him and will try to play a variety of roles in a number of diverse projects. He would also like to devote more time to writing and possibly direct, but will never give up acting.

Whatever the future holds, it's clear that David Duchovny has come a long way since abandoning his PhD at Yale. Despite her initial disapproval, his mother Margaret Ducovny is proud of her son's success. She currently works at a grade school in Manhattan and fol-lows David's career avidly, although the actor still senses that she would prefer him to be a 'distinguished university professor' rather than an actor and feels ashamed when she visits him on set! Every time Duchovny sees his mother, she asks him if he gets killed or appears naked in his next project. If the answer to either of those question is yes, she refuses to watch!

David Duchovny's long-term ambition is to have 'a wife and three kids'. His biggest fear is that he is typecast as Fox Mulder and becomes dependent on *X-Files* conventions and personal appearances to make a living!

For Gillian Anderson, *The X-Files* repre-sents 'the most joyous and the hardest time' of her life. As a result of the show, her life has changed irrevocably. Prior to landing the role of Dana Scully, she was unknown, single, vir-tually broke and had little experience of television work. By the end of her third year of the show, she was a financially-secure inter-national star and mother, with more than 60 hours of television to her credit.

Although she is known throughout the world as the sophisticated and straight-laced Dana Scully, Anderson feels that she has not completely lost her rebellious streak. She admits that she is intrigued by body piercing, but dare not try it whilst *The X-Files* are still being shot because 'the producers would have a fit'! Gillian would also love to have more children, but realises that she will have to wait until the show is off the air.

The actress still finds that *The X-Files* shooting schedule is remarkably hard, but wants to contribute a storyline or write a script at some point in the future, provided her work-load lightens.

Since 1995, Anderson has devoted more of her time to charitable causes. When she started to receive presents following Piper's birth, she eventually asked the fans to stop and donate some money to her favourite charity, The Neurofibromatosis Foundation, instead. The actress was subsequently asked to become their spokesperson. Anderson soon began to support various other charities, including those devoted to helping battered women and AIDS-victims, by attending fund-raising events and donating autographs for auction.

Anderson also started to campaign against sexual inequalities within the acting industry. She had learned all about that prob-lem when her *X-Files* co-star received a substantial pay rise at the beginning of the show's third year and decided to take a stand against the situation. She argues that men are higher paid than women, while women are judged simply by their looks and given less choice of roles than their male counterparts. 'Women in Hollywood are constantly shown that there's a difference between them and men, and that that's okay. But it's not okay,' she stated.

On the eve of her 28th birthday, Gillian Anderson declared that all her problems were behind her and proudly revealed that she had never felt better about her life. The actress believes that women grow up between the ages of 11 and 28, while men reach maturity a little later.

When *The X-Files* ceases production, Gillian Anderson probably won't leave Vancouver permanently. Her husband Clyde is a Canadian and her daughter Piper holds dual American/Canadian citizenship, so she expects to spend her time travelling back and

forth between Vancouver and Los Angeles.

Post-Dana Scully, the actress intends to pursue more stage roles and would also like to try her hand at a movie career. She admits to being terrified about her chances of success, and will probably test the waters by playing a small, supporting role in a movie before *The X-Files* ceases production. Anderson would like to appear in movies that 'have something to say, or say nothing extremely well, like *Pulp Fiction*.'

While it's true that Gillian Anderson was constantly overshadowed by David Duchovny during her time with *The X-Files*, it might actually work to her advantage in the long term. As a result of his high profile, Duchovny is in much more danger of being typecast than his co-star.

The actress' parents are ecstatic about their daughter's success, especially when they consider her troubled teenage years. Edward Anderson runs a successful post-production film facility, which he named 'Gillian' after his oldest daughter. Her mother Rosemary works as a computer analyst and is the biggest X-phile Gillian knows!

One of the proudest moments of Rosemary Anderson's life came during *The X-Files* third season hiatus, when she accompanied her daughter to the annual White House Press Corps dinner. During a discussion with President Clinton, Anderson revealed that she was a devoted Democrat supporter and agreed to participate in his upcoming Presidential campaign.

In one form or another, David Duchovny and Gillian Anderson look set to enjoy many more successes in the future. Both are extremely popular and talented performers, and should therefore be able to work in a wide variety of roles in diverse projects, provided that they avoid the pitfalls and perils of typecasting.

The X-Files, meanwhile, looks set to continue into the next millennium. As long as there are unsolved mysteries, unexplained phenomena and covert government activities, the public will clamour to see Fox Mulder and Dana Scully continue their search for the truth. Thus, in an uncertain world where trust is a thing of the past, the only thing you can be sure of is that David Duchovny and Gillian Anderson will be wearing Mulder and Scully's raincoats for many years to come.

Although *The X-Files* is due to cease production in early 1998, David Duchovny and Gillian Anderson's search for the truth is set to continue into the next millenium with a series of *X-Files* movies

▶ ▶

David Duchovny

New Year's Day

Working Girl

Bad Influence

Twin Peaks

The Rapture

Julia Has Two Lovers

Don't Tell Mom The Babysitter's Dead

Denial

Venice/Venice

Ruby

The Red Shoe Diaries (TV)

Chaplin

Beethoven

Baby Snatcher

Kalifornia

The X-Files (TV)

Space: Above and Beyond (TV)

Playing God

Gillian Anderson

Home Fires Burning

Class of '96 (TV)

The X-Files (TV)

Future Fantastic (TV)

▶▶